"Another great historical gem from one of the deans of presidential historians, Mike Purdy! Once again Purdy showcases the colorful humanity of the most powerful man on earth. A truly engaging and lively read!"

– **ROBERT BUCCELLATO**
Author of *Jimmy Carter in Plains*

"In his deeply researched book, Mike Purdy shows us two very different presidential friendships from a unique perspective – each other's eyes. While TR and Taft's friendship was founded on mutual affection, FDR and LBJ's was based upon symbiotic political expediency. Through his engaging writing style, Purdy effectively argues how the presidents, and indeed American and world history, would have been a lot different had they not had a little help from their friends."

– **LOUIS L. PICONE**
Author of *Grant's Tomb: The Epic Death of Ulysses S. Grant and the Making of an American Pantheon*

"Even when the nation is as closely divided as it is today, Mike Purdy's *Presidential Friendships* reminds us that the members of the nation's most exclusive club – the Presidents' Club – understand the importance of collaboration and compromise for the good of our country. This is a work that helps to restore our faith in the American democratic system."

– **LUKE A. NICHTER**
Author of *The Last Brahmin: Henry Cabot Lodge Jr. and the Making of the Cold War*

"*Presidential Friendships: How They Changed History* is a nifty book on several fronts. First and foremost, it is a good read! Mike Purdy is a fine storyteller! But perhaps even more important, he addresses the under-acknowledged substance of friendship, even for those at the top of the pecking order. We are getting a rare look into the personal aspects of four of our POTUSES, and you will enjoy it!"

– **FEATHER SCHWARTZ FOSTER**
Author of *The First Ladies* and
Mary Lincoln's Flannel Pajamas and Other Stories from the First Ladies' Closet

"Presidential historian Mike Purdy has produced a very perceptive, insightful analysis of the relationships of two sets of presidents in the 20th century---Theodore Roosevelt and William Howard Taft; and Franklin D. Roosevelt and Lyndon B. Johnson. Additionally, he brings attention in his introduction to other presidential friendships that have changed the course of American history, and are food for thought to be investigated in the future by Mike Purdy or other presidential scholars! This is certainly a topic ripe for expansion beyond the two relationships discussed here, and is a mine for those who are passionate as Purdy is about the American Presidency."

– DR. RONALD L. FEINMAN
Florida Atlantic University
Author of *Assassinations, Threats, and the American Presidency: From Andrew Jackson to Barack Obama*

"While it may be simpler to think of presidents in isolation, Mike Purdy offers an insightful and enjoyable examination at how the friendships (and in one case the feud) of two pairs of chief executives shaped both their presidencies and their legacies. A delightful and informative read."

– SHARON BOSTON
Creator and author of Nerd Trips (nerdtrips.net)

"Mike Purdy's *Presidential Friendships: How They Changed History* is a fresh perspective on the personalities of two of our most intriguing presidents. This examination of the unexpectedly close friendship between FDR, the patrician president, and LBJ, the cowboy congressman, reveals many interesting incidents and provides a compelling explanation for their unique relationship. The powerful charisma and big egos that both men had resulted in a mutual admiration society rather than a clash of the titans as might have been expected. A must read for any student of the presidency."

– PAUL M. SPARROW
Former Director
Franklin D. Roosevelt Presidential Library and Museum

ALSO BY MIKE PURDY

101 Presidential Insults:
What They Really Thought About Each Other –
and What It Means to Us

Grace in the Wilderness:
The Heart and Mind of Mike Purdy
(Selected Writings)

Volume 1 – Life and Work

Volume 2 – Family

Volume 3 – Theology

Volume 4 – History/Politics & Education

PRESIDENTIAL FRIENDSHIPS

How They Changed History

PRESIDENTIAL FRIENDSHIPS

How They Changed History

MIKE PURDY

PRESIDENTIAL HISTORY PRESS

Seattle • 2022

Refer all questions or inquiries to:
Mike Purdy
PO Box 46181
Seattle, WA 98146-0181

or by email to Mike@PresidentialHistory.com

www.PresidentialHistory.com/

Print ISBN: 978-1-66784-7-894
eBook ISBN: 978-1-66784-7-900

MIKE PURDY'S
PRESIDENTIALHISTORY.com

*To my friends of a lifetime as well as more recent ones,
near and far, who have walked with me on this joyful,
sometimes tearful, and uncertain journey of life.*

*You have enriched my life with your prayers, love,
encouragement, humor, wisdom, empathy, and support.*

*I've been privileged to walk with you as well in the
various seasons and situations of your lives.*

*That's what good friends do.
We make a difference for each other.*

You see, friends make everything better.[1]

GEORGE H.W. BUSH

CONTENTS

PREFACE

This book is a labor of love. It is the result of a lifetime of reading, research, and writing about the presidents dating back to my preteen years. Over the years, I've been fascinated to discover the personal connections our presidents had with one another, and how those friendships changed the contours of history.

Ideally, this book would be comprehensive and include stories of all presidential friendships (and feuds!). This has been my vision for decades as I've sought ways to humanize the presidents.

However, in May 2019, I was diagnosed with prostate cancer that has metastasized. This has launched me on an uncertain journey, and I'm all too aware in this season of life that my days are narrowing. Thus, it's important to me to publish this collection of stories about presidential friendships that I have written, and have it distributed to a wider audience of people who will appreciate and learn from these relationships – not only about history but about the foundational value of friendships.

Perhaps writing stories of other presidential friendships is something I may have time for and include in a future book. I've written unpolished stories of other presidential friendships. These are included in volume 4 of *Grace in the Wilderness: The Heart and Mind of Mike Purdy (Selected Writings)*.

Mike Purdy
Seattle, Washington
April 17, 2022 – Easter

ACKNOWLEDGMENTS

My daughter, Janet Purdy, provided the inspiration for me to publish this book with these two significant Roosevelt friendships and not wait for me to write the comprehensive book with stories about presidential friendships. She also provided key editorial assistance and ideas brainstorming about the book. This book would not be in your hands without her encouragement.

My son, David Purdy, designed the outstanding front and back covers of the book, and I'm grateful to him for lending his talents for the book. He blends amazing creativity with superb technical skills. It has been a pleasure to work with him on this book.

I am grateful for skilled editors who have helped make this a better book. I am indebted to my good friend, Clay Eals, for his outstanding editorial assistance in framing the book's introduction. His lifetime of writing and editing help me to be a better writer.

Adam Lumbley is also a skilled editor and careful reader whose valuable professional proofing and editorial suggestions significantly improved the quality of the book. I am indebted to him for his keen eye for corrections, proofing, style, word choices, and his deep appreciation of language.

Finally, I'm thankful for the encouragement from those who read my manuscript and were kind enough to write the endorsements that appear at the beginning of the book.

INTRODUCTION

American presidents belong to an exclusive club. Herbert Hoover joked that they make up a "trade union."[2]

While in crisis and pacing the quiet and historic halls of the White House presidents have gazed at portraits of their predecessors. They've wondered what George or Andy or Abe or Woodrow would have done.

Upon Richard Nixon's death in 1994, Bill Clinton said, "It's impossible to be in this job without feeling a special bond with the people who have gone before."[3]

Many of our presidents had even closer ties. They knew each other personally. These friendships opened new political opportunities that wouldn't otherwise exist, significantly shaping their mutual careers. They provided important continuity between administrations and generations.

In short, their relationships changed the course of history.

This book tells the story of two pairs of presidential friendships, each involving a Roosevelt who powerfully shaped and expanded the presidency in the 20th century.

Theodore Roosevelt (president from 1901 to 1909) and William Howard Taft (1909-1913) forged an early, fast friendship as young men serving in important federal positions in Washington, D.C., during the 1890s. The rambunctious Theodore rocked the boat as a member of the Civil Service Commission, while the reserved Taft approached his duties as solicitor general (representing the government's cases before the Supreme Court) with the dignity of a lawyer that was ingrained in his personality.

By temperament, personality, and politics they were an odd couple, but their friendship transcended their differences, and they supported and promoted each other for increasingly responsible government positions. It is no understatement that without this critical friendship, neither would have become president.

Sadly, politics and Theodore's ego fractured their friendship as Roosevelt challenged Taft, his handpicked successor, by seeking to reclaim the presidency he had loved so much. It's a dramatic human story full of warmth, ambition, and heartbreak.

Theodore's fifth cousin, Franklin D. Roosevelt (1933-1945), enjoyed a close relationship of political expediency with Lyndon B. Johnson (1963-1969) despite being separated by a generation and raised in dramatically different economic and geographic circumstances. FDR was a New York aristocrat, while LBJ was rooted in the poor Hill Country of Texas.

Surprisingly, their lives intersected for eight years during FDR's presidency when Johnson was a young New Deal official and later newly elected Texas congressman.

Both were master politicians and were driven by ambition. They knew how to amass and use power. They liked and saw themselves reflected in each other, almost as alter egos. FDR benevolently and instrumentally supported and shaped LBJ's emerging political career that eventually set him on a path to the White House. In turn, LBJ provided political intelligence and campaign contributions that helped Roosevelt win an unprecedented third term. "He was like a daddy to me,"[4] LBJ sobbed at FDR's death.

While this book is about these two significant Roosevelt relationships, they are far from the only presidential links that altered history. Here are nine other key presidential friendships that substantially shaped and changed the contours of American history:

Soldier and Bookworm – George Washington (1789-1797) and James Madison (1809-1817): The unlikely alliance between the magisterial and military Washington and the diminutive and scholarly Madison established critical governmental precedents in the republic's early days.

Confronter and Harmonizer – John Adams (1797-1801) and Thomas Jefferson (1801-1809): Tied together intimately in friendship as revolutionaries and diplomats in the nation's formative years, Adams and Jefferson eventually let politics fracture their warm relationship. Adams barely beat Jefferson for the presidency in 1796, and four years later Jefferson made Adams a one-term president. In their twilight years, they reconciled through correspondence initiated by Adams, who wrote, "You and I ought not to die before we have explained ourselves to each other."[5]

Friends and Political Partners – Thomas Jefferson and James Madison: For a half century, these founding giants enjoyed a close personal friendship and political partnership in the formation of the United States. Their strategic alliance was foundational for shaping the new nation.

Father and Son – John Adams and John Quincy Adams (1825-1829): One might say that John Quincy, the son of John, was raised to be president. All of the boy's political and diplomatic experiences and influences propelled him to the Executive Mansion in the hotly disputed election of 1824.

Great Engineer and the Man from Missouri – Herbert Hoover (1929-1933) and Harry S Truman (1945-1953): After a massive electoral defeat and repudiation by the voters in 1932, Hoover was a political pariah. His successor, FDR, ignored him, except to blame him. But when Truman assumed the presidency, he reached out to Hoover for assistance. Thus began a productive political partnership that crossed party lines and developed into a deep friendship in the winter of their lives.

Loveless Political Marriage – Dwight D. Eisenhower (1953-1961) and Richard M. Nixon (1969-1974): Eisenhower was genial and an immensely popular World War II hero. He picked 39-year-old freshman Sen. Richard Nixon as his running mate in 1952, launching Nixon's long national political career. In a tense moment of the campaign, Ike kept Dick on the ticket after the latter's famous Checkers speech in which he defended campaign contributions, including a dog. Their relationship was politically cordial and expedient, but never personally warm.

Tricky Dick and Boy Scout – Richard M. Nixon and Gerald R. Ford (1974-1977): Nixon and Ford were elected to Congress in the late 1940s, met early and began a personal and mutually beneficial political friendship that lasted 45 years. Comfortable with his friend, Nixon appointed Ford as vice president in 1973.

Rivalry and Reconciliation – Gerald R. Ford and Jimmy Carter (1977-1981): Ford and Carter waged a bitter 1976 presidential campaign full of personal defamation. Ford attacked his challenger as "cold and arrogant, even egotistical,"[6] while Carter contended that Ford was a "dormant, inactive President."[7] After they were both out of office they reconciled and forged, in Carter's words, "an intense personal friendship,"[8] cooperating in many ventures together.

Poppy and Bozo – George H. W. Bush (1989-1993) and Bill Clinton (1993-2001): Bush was defeated in 1992 by challenger Clinton, whom Bush labeled a "bozo."[9] Their political rivalry continued until natural disasters brought them together in their post-presidential years. They raised funds together to address catastrophes, creating a surprisingly warm personal friendship between the two ex-presidents.

These men, and other presidents, knew each other personally — many of them quite well. Their interactions have been significant, given that without these relationships, history would have veered in entirely different directions. These unique alliances have shaped our basic political protocols, how our government works, who eventually became president, and the success of humanitarian efforts.

Of course, the nature of these interactions often has fluctuated. Some ties have blown both hot and cold, between friendship and enmity, from civility to hostility, with and without reconciliation. Friendships have been ruined by vicious political campaigns. Goodwill and fellowship sometimes have eroded into verbal bloodbaths. Otherwise-reasonable men have impugned the motives of former colleagues, driving sharp and partisan wedges into once-sturdy bonds. Other relationships began with a lack of civility but warmed into genuine friendship and affection. Still others started and remained strong for years, even decades.

Presidential friendships undergird the adage that it is not what you know but who you know that makes a difference. Many businesses hire employees and get most of their work through personal connections. We join civic, social, and religious organizations to be connected to others. Even social media illustrate the centrality of relationships. We collect "friends" on Facebook, "connections" on LinkedIn, and "followers" on Twitter. All these ties open up doors of opportunity.

Presidential history is no different. The story of the Roosevelt connections told here highlights Woodrow Wilson's opinion that "friendship is the only cement that will ever hold the world together."[10] May these stories of presidential friendships inspire us and our leaders to intentionally cultivate relationships that transcend politics. Friendships change our lives and the course of history.

POLITICIAN AND JUDGE

Theodore Roosevelt and William Howard Taft

Mutual Trust and Admiration

(1890 – 1901)

W ill Taft turned around and waved good-bye to family and friends. He then hefted his full 250 pounds aboard the train and lumbered down the narrow aisle to take his seat. He was bound for Washington, D.C.

It should have been an exciting adventure for him. After all, he had just been appointed by President Benjamin Harrison as the nation's solicitor general. Instead, his mind was absorbed with anxiety, doubt, and a foreboding sense of loneliness.

He stared out the window, listening to the rhythmic clatter of the iron horse's wheels, and watching the familiar Ohio countryside disappear. With each passing mile, he sank deeper and deeper into an early mid-life crisis. Taft was just 32 years old, but he was sure that he had just derailed his promising career as a judge.

He had been born and raised in Cincinnati. It was home to him, a place where everybody knew him – a place where he felt comfortable and secure. Washington, on the other hand, was a "strange and forbidding city,"[11] according to his wife, Nellie. He knew very few people there, and he was convinced, according to his wife's later recollections, that "nobody wanted to know him."[12]

Taft had been seduced by the glamour of a political appointment in Washington, leading him to resign his very satisfying job as a judge in Cincinnati. He packed his bags for the capital. However much his heart longed for the measured life of a judge, the drama of politics ran in his blood. His father, Alphonso Taft, was undoubtedly pleased with the track his son's career was taking. Alphonso, now in his 80th year, had a long history of political involvement, having served as secretary of war and attorney general under President Ulysses Grant.

Regardless of how proud the senior Taft was of his son, Will continued to churn over and over in his mind whether he had made the right decision. After all, he didn't want to just *represent* the federal government in front of the U.S. Supreme Court as solicitor general. He wanted to *sit* on the high bench himself.

He understood it was an audacious hope for such a young lawyer. However, he had political connections. His friends back home encouraged him to cash in on his relationships to lobby Ohio's governor to talk with the president about such an appointment. Taft, however, was pessimistic about whether such a scheme would bear fruit, and as it turns out, he was right. Writing to his father, Taft realistically assessed his long shot odds of the coveted appointment: "My chances of going to the moon and of donning a silk gown at the hands of President Harrison are about equal."[13]

As the train rolled to its final stop, Will peered nervously out the window before leaving his seat. It was still dark outside at six o'clock in the morning of February 14, 1890. After fretting about his career for more than 500 miles, the normally upbeat Taft was as melancholy as the cold and gloomy Washington weather that day. No friends greeted him as he stepped off the train, adding to his feelings of insignificance. His wife, Nellie, later recalled that he felt "dismally unimportant in the midst of what seemed to him to be very formidable surroundings. He wondered to himself why on earth he had come."[14]

Just as loneliness is a breeding ground for insecurity, friendships are like seeds that blossom into self-confidence. The young Will Taft experienced both emotions in short order. His diffident entry into Washington soon gave way to a greater sense of self-assurance. Shortly after his arrival in the capital, the amiable Taft met and struck up a friendship with another young Harrison appointee, Theodore Roosevelt. This budding relationship helped allay Will's initial pessimism that no one would pay any attention to him or want to get to know him.

Roosevelt, who was about a year younger than Taft, had already been in Washington for nine months, quickly turning the low-profile job of U.S. Civil Service commissioner into a political lightning rod and launching pad for his own career. Unlike Taft's quiet and unnoticed entrance into the capital, Roosevelt burst into his new office on his first day and declared in his high-pitched, squeaky voice: "I am the new Civil Service Commissioner, Theodore Roosevelt of New York."[15] He then proceeded to bark out orders to a startled staff unaccustomed to such energy.

President Harrison sarcastically but accurately noted that the young commissioner "wanted to put an end to all evil in the world between sunrise and sunset."[16] Roosevelt possessed the zeal of an activist and was driven by a global-sized ego, a far cry from the more composed and conservative Taft who embodied the reserved heart of a legal scholar content to remain in the background.

Will and Theodore were an odd couple. Their personalities and styles were as different as night and day. Nevertheless, the relationship between the two young Republicans quickly blossomed into a warm friendship based on "mutual trust and admiration," according to one biographer.[17] Another biographer noted it was a friendship characterized by "an unusual relation of intimacy."[18]

The spark that fueled their friendship may have come from their Ivy League backgrounds – Roosevelt was a Harvard man while Taft hailed from Yale. Perhaps they enjoyed one another's company because they realized they were so different and complemented each other's differences. Or maybe their camaraderie was cemented by the freedom they both felt to confidentially share with the other their bold and ambitious dreams about the future: Taft longed to sit on the Supreme Court, and Roosevelt imagined living at 1600 Pennsylvania Avenue. Most likely, it was some combination of these elements that drew together these very different young political appointees.

Like all friendships, theirs was nurtured by the time they spent together. Taft settled into a house in the Dupont Circle neighborhood where Roosevelt had rented a house about a half-mile away.[19] They often tramped the roughly two miles to their offices together, engaged in animated conversation about politics, careers, and families. After a morning of hunkering down at their desks, they would continue their discussions over lunch.[20]

The tonic and comfort of their friendship, however, paled against the pursuit of their career aspirations. For two long years in Washington, Taft pined for putting on his judicial robes again. He missed presiding over a bench. When President Harrison dangled in front of him a judicial appointment to the federal Circuit Court of Appeals, Taft snatched at it. It was his ticket back home and a means to get his judicial career back on track. As Taft happily packed his bags for the next stop on what would be a long career in public service, he reluctantly bid farewell to his civil service commissioner friend.

Roosevelt remained in Washington for another four years until he too took a new job – as a police commissioner in New York City. There, for two very colorful and controversial years, he worked tirelessly to rid the police department of corruption and enforce existing laws. By 1896, Roosevelt had burned too many bridges in the Big Apple and his popularity was waning. He encountered stiff resistance for his efforts to enforce Sunday closure of saloons on the only day when the working class could socialize over drinks. TR began casting his eye about for a new political appointment to get himself out of the no-win police job.

He decided to capitalize on his knowledge and reputation as an amateur military strategist. More than a dozen years earlier, when he was still in his early twenties, Roosevelt had researched and written a scholarly and highly acclaimed book on the naval war of 1812 – still considered the definitive work on the subject today. He grandly set his sights on getting appointed as assistant secretary of the Navy.

Unfortunately, at least one major obstacle stood in his way – the job was already filled by someone else. Democrat William McAdoo held the keys to the office, courtesy of his appointment by President Grover Cleveland in 1893. And if the Democrats renewed their lease on the White House in the 1896 election, Roosevelt would be out of luck in his quest to move back to Washington. He knew that his only chance of possibly snagging the Navy job was if a Republican was elected president in November. Roosevelt decided to do his part to help influence the election.

He enthusiastically threw himself into the presidential campaign of the Republican nominee, William McKinley. Roosevelt rode the rails throughout the west, captivating audiences at countless whistle-stops with his energetic and teeth-chomping speeches, urging voters to cast their ballots for the former Ohio governor. He hoped that McKinley, if elected, would take appreciative notice of his electioneering efforts and reward him with the coveted appointment.

Public campaigning for McKinley wasn't Roosevelt's only strategy in his crusade to be tapped for the Navy position. He also launched a stealth campaign to shape and improve McKinley's less than positive impressions of him. This behind-the-scenes initiative would be carried out by a loyal network of well-connected friends and influential acquaintances that Roosevelt had amassed over the years. If ever there was a time to call in favors, it was now.

As Roosevelt mentally canvassed which of his friends knew McKinley, or had access to the candidate, he doubtless smiled when he recalled that Will Taft and McKinley both hailed from the Buckeye State. More importantly for Roosevelt, the politically connected Taft had the candidate's ear. Here was an old and faithful friend who could perhaps persuade McKinley that Roosevelt was the right man for the Navy Department.

When Taft swung through New York City in the spring of 1896, the judge and the cop eagerly reunited over a meal together, catching up on years of politics, careers, and families. Roosevelt painted a vivid picture for Taft of the brewing tensions with the New York City police job. He shared his desire to escape city politics and capture the Navy position in Washington. Taft agreed to lend his weight for his old friend by talking with McKinley and urging him to appoint Roosevelt as assistant secretary.

Unfortunately, Roosevelt's reputation with McKinley was unfavorable and he viewed TR as an excitable and unpredictable character. "The truth is, Will," McKinley candidly revealed to Taft, "Roosevelt is always in such a state of mind."[21]

Even with the lobbying by Taft and other friends of Theodore, it was an uphill battle to convince the reluctant McKinley. The relationship between Roosevelt and McKinley had never been warm. It simmered just below professionally cordial. Roosevelt knew that he was not one of McKinley's favorites,[22] and McKinley was certainly not one of Roosevelt's favorites either. Years earlier, Roosevelt had opposed McKinley's bid to become speaker of the House, and McKinley still felt a bitter taste in his mouth over Roosevelt's recent backing of another candidate for the 1896 presidential nomination.

It would also be a hard sell to convince the peaceful McKinley that the combative Roosevelt wouldn't overstep his bounds in the Navy job. To one Roosevelt fan attempting to influence McKinley after the election, the president-elect expressed his doubts and concerns about appointing Roosevelt. "I want peace," McKinley said, "and I am told that your friend Theodore – whom I know only slightly – is always getting into rows with everybody. I am afraid he is too pugnacious."[23]

Ultimately, however, Roosevelt's intensive whistle-stopping and networking campaign were sufficient to twist the new president's arm. Will Taft and other friends brought TR over the finish line. Just a month after McKinley's inauguration on March 4, 1897,[24] the president tapped Roosevelt as assistant secretary of the Navy, allowing Roosevelt to bolt from what was becoming an increasingly untenable political situation in New York City.

The Navy berth lasted just over a year and Roosevelt began a meteoric rise to power. In four short years, he rapidly transformed himself from Navy bureaucrat to national war hero to governor of New York, before his 1901 incarnation as vice-president for McKinley's second term.

It was from this new position as second in line to the presidency that Roosevelt privately sought to audition Will Taft on the stage of world politics. Notably, there was one big difference between Roosevelt's new lobbying efforts and Taft's earlier influence in helping Roosevelt land the Navy job. Taft was very content with his lifetime appointment as a federal appeals court judge in Ohio, while Roosevelt had been desperate to get out of New York City politics. There was only one job that Taft really coveted, and he hoped that his growing reputation as a jurist would soon land him an appointment to the U.S. Supreme Court.

Despite Taft's judicial hopes, Roosevelt and officials in the McKinley administration (not to mention Taft's wife) had other designs for Taft's career that would ultimately take the judge on a twenty-year detour before he finally achieved his lifelong ambition of serving on the Supreme Court.

As the new century dawned, President McKinley wrestled with how his administration should manage and govern the newly acquired Philippine Islands. In a world still absorbed in a colonial chess game between global powers, Spain had ceded the archipelago to the United States in late 1898 for $20 million. The territorial transfer of the islands was part of the treaty that ended the Spanish-American War. McKinley finally decreed that a governor-general should be appointed to establish and administer a colonial government on the islands. Establishing the position was easy. The more difficult task would be to find a man of stature with the right combination of skills, knowledge, and personality who could shape the job and ease McKinley's migraine of managing the islands.

Vice President Roosevelt, always a quick thinker with an opinion about everything, knew exactly what lofty executive and judicial qualifications would be needed by the governor-general. The governor-general, he wrote "ought to combine the qualities which would make a first-class President of the United States with the qualities which would make a first-class chief justice of the United States."[25] And not surprisingly Roosevelt also had a ready recommendation for the man who met this high standard. Taft was, he wrote, "the only man he knew who possessed all these qualities."[26]

On July 4, 1901, McKinley agreed and named Taft as the first Governor-General of the islands. Without the Roosevelt-Taft friendship, Taft would have remained as a judge and never been tapped for this or other increasingly responsible positions. Roosevelt was delighted to see his old friend chosen for the important post and congratulated Taft, raving that he was "one of the very few men instead of being fit for only one job is able to do well almost any job which needs to be done."[27]

Roosevelt's effusive praise of Taft continued as Taft executed his work in the Philippines: "A more high-minded and disinterested man does not live; and he represents as high-minded and disinterested, aye, and as successful, an effort to keep a people as any recorded in history."[28]

By the time Taft returned to Washington six months after his appointment to report on his progress in the Philippines, Roosevelt was president, having assumed the office upon McKinley's assassination in September. Despite their politically important and personal friendship of more than a decade, hints of their differences began to seep through slowly developing cracks in the relationship.

Taft privately voiced concerns about Roosevelt's weaknesses as well as his own irritation with the president. A little over a month after Roosevelt became president, Taft assessed the new president's performance, telling his brother, Harry, that Roosevelt did not have "the capacity for winning people to his support that McKinley had."[29] Taft also confided to a friend that he wished Theodore "would not think out loud so much,"[30] a mannerism that grated on Taft's deliberative judicial temperament.

While in Washington, the governor-general testified before the Senate and consulted with the president. Roosevelt commissioned Taft to meet with Pope Leo XIII, to persuade the pontiff to sell farmland the church owned in the islands. Never shy about self-promotion, the President also commissioned Taft to present the Roman Catholic leader with a personal gift from Roosevelt: an eight-volume set of the prolific president's writings. Always the good soldier and faithful friend, Taft delivered the books to the pope, perhaps inwardly cringing over his role in helping inflate his boss' already supersized ego.[31]

Power Partnership

(1902 – 1907)

Like father, like son. Taft and his father, Alphonso, were both attorneys and judges. Both received prominent presidential appointments. And they both sought and longed for an appointment to the Supreme Court. For Alphonso, that dream never materialized.[32]

In 1902, the younger Taft was approached by his friend, the president, who offered him what had eluded the elder Taft – the rare opportunity of a coveted appointment to the high court. "You can at this juncture," Roosevelt wrote, "do far better service on [the] Supreme Court than any other man." Taft had struck gold, and Roosevelt was delighted with the privilege of offering to elevate his good friend to the high court. It was a way for the president to fulfill the audacious dream that Taft had shared with him a dozen years earlier, when their careers were just being launched in Washington. "I feel that your duty is on the Court unless," the president playfully jabbed, "you have decided not to adopt [a] judicial career."[33]

It should have been an obvious and easy decision for Taft. His heart and temperament *were* fixed on a judicial career. A prized seat on the Supreme Court while only in his mid-40s would be an early capstone to his legal career. It would ensure him with a long and hopefully influential tenure on the bench. However, the decision wasn't easy for Taft.

Despite the fact that he could almost taste the pending appointment that would fulfill a goal that had eluded him and his father before him, Taft was also an incredibly conscientious and responsible public official. He felt that the "gravity of the situation"[34] in the Philippines prevented him from leaving as governor-general. There were still too many pressing issues that he wanted to see through to completion. There was also pressure from his wife and other members of his family who wanted to see him pursue the presidency, and who felt that the Supreme Court would not help promote his political career.

With a sense of duty to public service above his own self-interests, Taft informed the president in an October 28, 1902 telegram that he was reluctantly declining the appointment "even if it is certain that it can never be repeated."[35]

Incredibly, the offer was repeated. By chance, another Supreme Court vacancy occurred before the year was out, and Roosevelt once again offered the position to Taft.[36] More than an offer this time, the president virtually commanded Taft in a November 26, 1902 letter to leave the Philippines and take a seat on the court. "I am awfully sorry, old man," TR wrote Taft, but "I find that I shall have to bring you home and put you on the Supreme Court."[37]

Poor Taft. He had already agonized over this painful decision just months earlier, and now he had to re-think his decision yet again. Once again, the governor-general was sorely tempted by the opportunity to fulfill his lifelong ambition. And yet not much had changed in the last few months. He still felt constrained by his duty in the Philippines, despite health challenges he was facing. In a January 7, 1903[38] message to the president, Taft made "one more appeal" to the president on the basis of "our personal friendship," and outlined why it was important for him to remain in the Philippines.[39] And so he tempted fate yet a second time, politely declining the position.

"All right," TR shot back. "Stay where you are. I shall appoint some one else to the Court."[40] It was not an easy pill for the president to swallow. Roosevelt felt a certain amount of pride in, and even political ownership of Taft. He had been partially responsible for lifting the otherwise obscure judge out of Ohio and depositing him on the world stage in the Philippines. He knew of Taft's longing to serve on the Supreme Court, and he had it within his power to fulfill Taft's dreams. TR was mystified when Taft didn't automatically and enthusiastically pack his bags for Washington.

Undoubtedly, Roosevelt was also somewhat offended by the challenge to his presidential authority. After all, he had told Taft that, as president, he sees "the whole field," and it was his responsibility to "put the men on whom he most relies in the particular positions in which he himself thinks they can render the greatest public good."[41] Taft had bucked and challenged the presumption that the president knows best. As much as TR respected the lovable Taft for his sense of duty, he sensed a certain amount of control slipping from between his fingers when Taft demonstrated that he was his own man by making a decision based on what was best for the Philippines, and not just Taft's personal self-interest. Nevertheless, Roosevelt's high regard for his friend remained unchanged, prompting him to declare a few months later: "I wonder if you realize how much I respect and admire you!"[42]

Less than three months after Taft declined the president's second offer of a seat on the Supreme Court, the persistent TR came knocking again on his friend's door, even more insistently – this time entreating him to follow in his father's footsteps and serve as secretary of war as soon as Elihu Root left the post, scheduled to occur within the year. Aware of Taft's dedication and commitment to the Philippines, Roosevelt coaxingly flattered him: "No one can quite take your place as Governor, but no one of whom I can now think save only you can at all take Root's place as Secretary."[43]

For a variety of personal and political reasons, Taft was now more inclined to give heed to the president's wishes. Perhaps the chief factor was the support of his wife, which had been absent with the enticements to a Supreme Court appointment. The opinionated and controlling Nellie exercised a strong hand in the direction of her husband's career. She had never been keen about Will serving on the Supreme Court. He should be president and she feared that the court would sideline his career. The War Department, however, was more pleasing to her, because, as she recalled after Taft's presidency, "it was in line with the kind of work I wanted my husband to do, the kind of career I wanted for him and expected him to have."[44]

With marital opposition to the cabinet position melting, Taft turned his attention to money – the cost of living in Washington was high, especially for a cabinet member expected to entertain. Taft wrote the president about his concerns.

TR downplayed the financial burden and encouraged Taft to "live just exactly as you and I did"[45] in the early 1890s when they had first met and lived in Washington. "So, old man," Roosevelt wrote, "it would really add immensely to my pleasure as an American to have you, who will be the foremost member of my Cabinet in the public eye, live the simplest kind of life."[46] Ultimately, a commitment from Taft's family to make up the difference in expenses did more to convince Taft than did the president's proposed austerity program.

With marital and money concerns addressed, there was also the matter of Taft's health to consider. The Philippines had been hard on the overweight Taft physically, and TR capitalized on this in his campaign to convince Taft to come to Washington: "Seriously concerned for your health," the president wrote.

Finally, one of Taft's sticking points with the Supreme Court appointments had been that he would be unable to finish up the important work he had begun in the Philippines. With the secretary of war position, he would still be able to impact the development of the islands, which would be under his general oversight. He would also have until the end of the year to tie up loose ends in the Philippines before moving to Washington.

Thus, Taft relented and accepted the president's forceful invitation to come to Washington. Roosevelt was delighted. The president eagerly looked forward to renewing his friendship with Taft. TR wrote to his son, Ted, that "Taft is a splendid fellow and will be an aid and comfort in every way."[47]

At the end of December 1903, Taft's ship steamed away from Manila. A month later, on February 1, 1904, he reported for duty at his new post, beginning what would become a four-year stint as secretary of war. He was pleasantly surprised at Roosevelt's enthusiasm of working with him: "The President seems really to take much comfort that I am in his Cabinet," Will wrote to Nellie who was spending the winter in the California sun. "He tells me so and then he tells people who tell me."[48]

After a little over a month of working closely with Theodore for the first time in their careers, Taft was impressed with the president. He praised him in a letter to Nellie, his words containing just a lightly veiled hint of TR's sometimes volatile personality. Theodore "is a very sweet and natural man and a very trusting man *when he believes in one.* I am growing to be very fond of him."[49]

As a cabinet member and close friend of the president's, Will and Nellie "dined frequently at the White House,"[50] according to Taft family biographer Ishbel Ross. Roosevelt was quite pleased with his new secretary of war, commenting that "he is, of course, the greatest imaginable comfort to me here, and I think the only man in the country who could have taken Root's place."[51]

Not only was TR immensely satisfied with Taft's performance in the War Department, but the president also turned to Taft in early 1905 to fill in as acting secretary of state during John Hay's illness. He put Taft virtually in charge of the government when a vacation beckoned the president away from Washington for five weeks. In the president's words, he would leave "the burdens of state on Taft's broad shoulders."[52] Again, Taft's performance pleased his friend and boss immensely: "I think you are keeping the lid on in great shape!"[53]

In early 1906, with yet another vacancy on the Supreme Court to fill, Roosevelt once again turned to his favorite friend and trusted colleague and offered Taft an associate justiceship. For the third time in four years, Taft was again torn with the dilemma of duty versus desire.

The most rewarding and fulfilling times of his professional career had clearly been the years he had served as a judge. His personality and psychological make-up were a good match with a judicial career, not an administrative or political one. For at least twenty years, he had dreamed about serving on the Supreme Court, and now, once again, thanks to his friendship with the president, it was his for the taking.

However, Taft's strong sense of civic duty once again blocked his path. Clearly, there were things he wanted to bring to conclusion in the Philippines and Panama in his role as secretary of war. "I looked into my motives," Taft told the president, "and saw that what I was about to do [accept the Supreme Court job] was the result of a desire to avoid controversies that were mine to fight and that it was my duty to my Filipino friends...to stay and fight them."[54]

In addition, Taft's decision-making process was complicated again by the strong and controlling voices of Nellie and his extended family who continued to wield heavy influence in shaping his career. They were still holding out for getting him elected president. An associate justiceship on the Supreme Court would thwart those plans. Had the job offer been that of chief justice, Taft might have overruled his family, conquered his civic duty conscience, and accepted the position.[55]

With great reluctance and a divided heart, Taft thanked the president for his vote of confidence, but informed Roosevelt he preferred to continue his work with the War Department.

Knowing Taft's long-term dream of serving on the Supreme Court, TR was understandably baffled by his friend's response:

> You say that it is your decided personal preference to continue your present work. This I had not understood. On the contrary, I gathered that what you really wanted to do was to go on the bench, and that my urging was in the line of your inclination, but in a matter in which you were in doubt as to your duty.[56]

It was becoming increasingly clear to many that Taft was being groomed as Roosevelt's heir apparent. Taft understood that to refuse a Supreme Court appointment for the third time would cause some people to question his motives. Taft was confident that Theodore understood his motives, as well his desire to serve on the court rather than as president. Taft wrote the president at the end of July 1906:

> I know that few, if any, even among my friends will credit me with anything but a desire, unconscious perhaps, to run for the Presidency and that I must face and bear this misconstruction of what I do. But I am confident that you credit my reasons as I give

them to you and will believe me when I say I would much prefer to go on the Supreme Bench for life than to run for the Presidency and that in twenty years of judicial service I could make myself more useful to the country than as President even if the impossible event of my election should come about.[57]

While TR would have been delighted to elevate Taft to the Supreme Court, he benefited by the continued partnership with Taft as secretary of war. Working well together professionally, Taft faithfully administered the president's policies, even though he often encountered difficulties in the process. In a letter to Taft during the summer of 1906, Roosevelt wrote that he admired Taft more than any man, except Lincoln and Washington, and took some devious delight in seeing Taft sometimes get into "hot water" just as he did himself:

One element in my enjoyment was, as it always is with you, my unchristian delight in finding that you, whom I admire as much not only as any public man of the present but as any public man of the past, bar Lincoln and Washington – indeed, whom I suppose I admire more than any other public man, but these two – get into just the same kind of hot water from time to time that I get into myself. The water is not as hot, and you never deserve to have gotten into it, as I am sorry to say I abundantly do; but it is a comfort to feel that the man I love and admire and respect encounters the difficulties that I encounter.[58]

Roosevelt and Taft made an effective team and the president was indebted to Taft for his loyalty and effectiveness in carrying out the administration's policies. Writing to the British historian Sir George Otto Trevelyan, Roosevelt acknowledged Taft's strengths and his debt to him:

He is the man through whom I have been doing my work about the Panama Canal. He has no more fear in dealing with the interests of great corporate wealth than he has in dealing with the leaders of the most powerful labor unions; and if either go wrong he has not the slightest hesitation in antagonizing them. To strength and courage, clear insight, and practical common sense, he adds a very noble and disinterested character...He helps me in every way more than I can say...[59]

Not only did Roosevelt value Taft's effectiveness but he considered Will Taft to be "the most lovable personality [he had] ever come in contact with."[60] Despite their differing personalities and styles, Theodore and Will continued their warm friendship that had been nurtured in the early years of their careers in Washington. The president insightfully recognized that Taft brought "stability and serenity"[61] to the administration, in marked contrast to the Rough Rider's own style.

Presidential Transition

(1908)

The mood at the White House was festive and celebratory on the evening of November 8, 1904. Encouraging election returns poured in from coast to coast. The votes demonstrated that President Roosevelt was winning, as an ebullient TR crowed to his son Kermit, "the greatest popular majority and the greatest electoral majority ever given a candidate for President."[62] The President was ecstatic and delighted with the enthusiastic show of support from across the country. He turned to his wife, Edith, and proudly declared that he was "no longer a political accident."[63]

Then, in his moment of supreme triumph, catapulted by the voters into his own full term of office, Roosevelt uttered words he would come to painfully regret – words that would haunt him for the rest of his life. The president's rash decision about his future would change the course of history and reverberate across the American political landscape and around the world for decades to come. Most tragically, TR's fateful decision that night would eventually sow seeds of discord, leading to the disintegration of his long-term and close friendship with Will Taft.

To the reporters assembled that night at the White House to cover election returns, the president spoke these noble, yet ill-advised words:

> On the 4th of March next I shall have served three and a half years and this constitutes my first term. The wise custom which limits the president to two terms regards the substance and not the form; and under no circumstances will I be a candidate for or accept another nomination.[64]

Having taken himself out of the running in 1908, the president nevertheless wanted to shape that election and install a successor who would faithfully carry out the policies and initiatives he had begun. He began to cast his eye about, critically evaluating the leading Republicans of the day. Elihu Root, Roosevelt's first secretary of war and later secretary of state, was a highly regarded attorney, but was unwilling to be dragged through a political campaign. Charles Evans Hughes, a Supreme Court justice, was seen as a possible contender. Taft was also a possible heir apparent, even though Taft had stated in 1904 that the thought of "a national campaign for the presidency is to me a nightmare."[65]

For his part, Taft would have been perfectly satisfied with the president tapping Hughes, telling the president that if he picked Hughes, "you may be sure that you will awaken no feeling of disappointment on my part...it will leave not the slightest trace of disappointment."[66] In fact, Taft must have secretly hoped that Hughes would be Roosevelt's choice. Not only would it keep Taft from living out the nightmare of a political campaign, but it would open up Hughes' seat on the high court. Maybe lightning would strike a fourth time and Taft would again be offered an appointment to the Supreme Court.

However much Taft might have dreamed of such a turn of events, he still had to deal with his opinionated and politically ambitious wife, Nellie. Even though Taft didn't have the stomach for the presidency, Nellie was relentlessly pushing him in that direction. She was driven by a vow she had made a quarter century ago as a teenager. She had been inspired by a visit to the Rutherford B. Hayes White House with her father. She resolved then and there that she would only marry a man who might one day become president. She hitched her star to Will Taft as her ticket back to the glamour of the White House.

One evening, after Will and Nellie had enjoyed a dinner at the White House with the president, they moved to the library for further conversation. Roosevelt was still mulling over in his mind who to throw his weight behind as his successor. TR was in a playful mood, and began to chant to his guests:

"I am the seventh son of a seventh daughter. I have clairvoyant powers. I see a man before me weighing three hundred and fifty pounds. There is something hanging over his head. I cannot make out what it is; it is hanging by a slender thread. At one time it looks like the presidency - then again it looks like the chief justiceship."

"Make it the presidency!" Nellie immediately jumped in.

"Make it the chief justiceship," Taft said hopefully and longingly.[67]

Given his high respect and admiration for Taft, and the close personal friendship they had enjoyed for almost twenty years, Roosevelt ultimately made up his mind to anoint his secretary of war for the 1908 Republican nomination. After spending an evening in May 1906 with the president, Taft reported blandly and without much enthusiasm to his wife, "I went to the White House for a long talk with the president...He thinks I am the one to take his mantle."[68] Despite his concerns about a national campaign, let alone the presidency itself, Taft was a good soldier and a good husband, and went along with the desires of his fan club.

With Roosevelt's immense popularity as president, his selection of Taft to succeed him virtually assured Taft he would be nominated at the Republican convention in June, 1908. After Taft effortlessly captured the nomination, the president gushed privately: "Always excepting Washington and Lincoln, I believe that Taft as president will rank with any other man who has ever been in the White House."[69] It was to prove a woefully inaccurate prophecy, colored by Roosevelt's almost blind admiration for Taft.

Publicly, Roosevelt also issued a strong statement of support for his hand-picked successor, and predicted what kind of president Taft would be:

> I do not believe there can be found in the whole country a man so well fitted to be President. He is not only absolutely fearless, absolutely disinterested and upright, but he has the widest acquaintances with the nation's needs without and within and the broadest sympathies with all our citizens. He would be as emphatically a President of the plain people as Lincoln, yet not Lincoln himself would be freer from the least taint of demagogy, the least tendency to arouse or appeal to any class hatred of any kind.[70]

Roosevelt admired and viewed his portly friend as a virtual clone of himself. The president viewed his selection of Taft as a means to extend his influence into the next administration. TR grandiosely proclaimed that Taft was "a man whose theory of public and private duty is my own, and whose practice of this theory is what I hope mine is…if we can elect him president we achieve all that could be achieved by continuing me in the office."[71]

The president's assessment about Taft was flawed and clouded by their friendship. Yes, Taft was a faithful administrator under Roosevelt, but as president, he would make different policy decisions than TR would have made. TR's giddy and unrealistically glowing confidence in Taft would eventually lead to a bitter political feud between the two men when the former president began to realize that he could no longer control the puppet friend he had mentored for years.

For much of the 1908 presidential campaign, Roosevelt was in a positively jovial mood, cheering Taft onto victory, and offering words of encouragement. However, the somewhat reluctant Taft was not enjoying himself on the campaign trail – it was proving to be the nightmare he had prophesied it would be four years earlier. A month after the convention, TR wrote the nominee from Oyster Bay: "Poor old boy! Of course you are not enjoying the campaign. I wish you had some of my bad temper. It is at times a real aid to enjoyment."[72] Notably though, Taft had none of the fire and drive that marked the Rough Rider.

Such differences between the two friends, however, failed to dampen TR's enthusiastic admiration for Taft, and his expectation that Taft would go down in history as one of the presidential greats. In August 1908, Roosevelt wrote: "You blessed old trump, I have always said you would be the greatest President, bar only Washington and Lincoln, and I feel mightily inclined to strike out the exceptions!"[73]

At the heart of Roosevelt's praise was his attempt to ensure his own place in the history books. In his mind, unconsciously perhaps, was the thought that if he could create, mentor, and anoint the greatest president ever, then he too would go down in history as a great president for having recognized and nurtured the embryonic leadership of his friend, and for having gifted the nation with such a man.

By September, the head cheerleader was offering his advice to Taft on how to make a good impression in the campaign and deal with the Democratic nominee, William Jennings Bryan:

> Hit them hard, old man! Let the audience see you smile always, because I feel that your nature shines out so transparently when you do smile – you big, generous, high-minded fellow…The trouble is that you would always rather fight for a principle or for a friend than for yourself. Now hit at them; challenge Bryan on his record…Do not answer Bryan; attack him! Don't let *him* make issues and never define your religious belief.[74]

Only 50 years old and still full of energy in the waning days of the campaign, Roosevelt surely felt ongoing pangs of regret for having rashly taken himself out of the race four years earlier. To compensate, Roosevelt lived vicariously through Taft's campaign – tying Taft's success to his own and viewing Taft's victory as a continuation of the Roosevelt administration.

"He and I view public questions exactly alike," the almost fatherly Roosevelt blindly boasted. "In fact, I think it is very rare that two public men have ever been so much at one in all the essentials of their public beliefs."[75]

Despite the wearing rigors of the campaign, Taft was grateful to his long-time friend, for whom he had the greatest respect. As the ballots were tabulated on November 3, it became increasingly clear that Taft had won a resounding victory. The tired president-elect declared to his supporters his hope that his administration would be a "worthy successor to that of Theodore Roosevelt."[76]

In the aftermath of the 1908 election, Roosevelt made preparations for an upcoming African safari. With a forced joviality to mask his sadness of leaving the presidency, he wrote to the president-elect: "Ha ha! *You* are making up your Cabinet. *I*, in a light hearted way, have spent the morning testing the rifles for my African trip. Life has compensations!"[77] In reality, Roosevelt would have given almost anything to be in Taft's position, instead of preparing to give up the reins of power and the job he had enjoyed so much.

On New Year's Day, 1909, Roosevelt telegraphed his best wishes to the man he had tapped as his successor: "We believe that the coming years will be very happy for you and we know that through you they will be years of benefit to our people."[78] While the president's hopeful sentiment was genuine, it was based more on what Roosevelt had experienced in the White House, than how Taft might respond. Unfortunately, Taft's years as president were lonely and unpleasant ones.[79]

The Break in the Relationship

(1909 – 1911)

In the months after Taft's election and before his inauguration, rumors were scurrying their way around Washington that the fabled Roosevelt-Taft friendship had hit a rocky spot. From Taft's perspective, all was still well, and in public Roosevelt generally maintained the facade that the relationship was strong. Inside though, Roosevelt was beginning to seethe. It all began for Roosevelt a few days after Taft's election victory.

As might be expected, given all that Roosevelt had done in handing the presidency to Taft on a silver platter, the grateful president-elect thanked his friend. He sent TR a letter on November 7th expressing his gratitude for all the president's efforts in vaulting him into the presidency. The letter was an honest, innocent, and well-meaning gesture by Taft – but it was also clumsy, tactless, and too brutally honest to share with a man whose ego continued to expand faster than the exploding universe.

While Taft was an efficient administrator, his legendary lack of political finesse did not always serve him well. The president-elect thoughtlessly inserted four unnecessary and inflammatory words in his message to the president – words that would prove to be a first trickle of foul water seeping through the otherwise solid dam of the longstanding friendship of the two men.

Taft wrote to the outgoing president that "my selection and election are chiefly your work." And had Taft stopped there, all would have been well. His next sentence, however, not only backfired but set off fireworks: "You and my brother Charley made that possible which in all probability would not have occurred otherwise."[80] Taft's faux pas was that he had naively elevated his brother Charley, who had helped raise funds for the campaign, to the same level as the president. Roosevelt, with his colossal ego that needed to be individually and consistently stroked, was personally offended and deeply wounded.

Roosevelt had mentored Taft and given him most of his major career breaks. He had created Taft. He had made him president. To suggest that anyone else was primarily responsible for Taft's election, demonstrated to TR a total lack of gratitude. Roosevelt was incensed by Taft's letter and boiled inside. After a congressman congratulated Roosevelt on his success in picking his successor and getting him elected, TR's anger erupted, and he sputtered:

He mentions his brother Charles in connection with me? Does he not know that I could have beaten him, had I not been for him? Is he not aware of the fact that I could easily have taken that nomination myself? The idea of his putting his brother Charles alongside me in an expression of gratitude...It is monstrous, I tell you.[81]

In one sense, Roosevelt never got over that letter. Even without the blunder of the letter, the dynamics of their relationship would have naturally morphed as their roles shifted. For years, Taft had faithfully served Roosevelt as his loyal lieutenant, conscientiously implementing the president's policies and directives. Taft's election as president signaled a necessary change in the relationship. Roosevelt found it hard to accept this – that the man he had chosen for the presidency would actually be president, while he would fade into the background as an ex-president.

Roosevelt craved power and loved being president. He loved being the center of attention, or as his outspoken daughter Alice Roosevelt Longworth bluntly observed: "He always wanted to be the corpse at every funeral, the bride at every wedding, and the baby at every christening." When his successor began to steal the limelight and Roosevelt found himself relegated to the sidelines, he was childishly miffed. Roosevelt's good friend and British ambassador, Sir Cecil Spring Rice, insightfully noted during Roosevelt's presidency that "you must always remember that the president is about six"[82] years old.

It would certainly have been more palatable for Roosevelt to acknowledge the changing dynamics of his relationship with Taft if the president-elect's letter had been more deferential and exclusively appreciative of Roosevelt in single handedly making Taft president.

To most casual observers, as Taft's inauguration day approached, the relationship between the two men appeared as strong as ever. Since the election, however, the rumblings of a slowly growing rift between them, attributable in large measure to Taft's insensitive letter and Roosevelt's hyper-sensitive response, was the underground buzz in Washington.

Despite the rage that continued to boil inside Roosevelt, the president graciously invited Will and Nellie as his guests in the White House on his last night there before Taft's March 4, 1909 inauguration. Taft, still oblivious that his words had drawn blood, replied to his friend and mentor and boss:

> People have attempted to represent that you and I were in some way at odds during this last three months, whereas you and I know that there has not been the slightest difference between us and I welcome the opportunity to stay the last night of your administration under the White House roof to make as emphatic as possible the refutation of any such suggestion.[83]

From Taft's perspective, the relationship was still strong, and he signed the letter with genuine warmth: "With love and affection, my dear Theodore."[84]

The dinner that night at the White House, however, didn't go well. Although Theodore and Will were in good spirits, tensions were high between their wives. Taft later recalled the night as the "dreadful dinner the Roosevelts gave us."[85]

On inauguration day, Theodore and Will good-naturedly joshed with one another about the weather and which one could claim ownership of a brutal snowstorm that had ravaged Washington overnight. Roosevelt jokingly claimed that "as soon as I am out where I can do no further harm to the Constitution," the storm will be over.[86] Taft, who always had mixed emotions about becoming president, quickly and brilliantly retorted "You're wrong. It is my storm. I always knew it would be a cold day when I became President."[87] In one sense, the snowstorm was a precursor of the blizzard that would soon bury the once warm and convivial relationship between the two men.

The snow was still falling as their horse-drawn carriage slowly made its way down the snow and ice laden Pennsylvania Avenue to the Capitol for the oath of office ceremonies – held inside in the Senate chambers as a concession to the weather. When Taft finished his inaugural address, the former president warmly and vigorously extended his hand and offered words of congratulations. Taft later told Nellie that TR had said: "God bless you, old man. It is a great state document."[88] A reporter nearby recalled that Roosevelt's praise was more exalted than Taft had reported: "That is the greatest inaugural address that has been delivered since Lincoln took the oath of office."[89]

Citizen Roosevelt made his way back home to Sagamore Hill, but he struggled with giving up the power of the presidency. "I have had a bully time and enjoyed every hour of my presidency," he told friends.[90] Deep down, he was still irked by Taft's letter that put him and Charley Taft on the same level. The oblivious new president, however, was apparently still unaware of the brewing firestorm he had created with his graceless letter of gratitude after the election.

Shortly after his inauguration, Taft wrote an article for *Colliers* magazine entitled "My Predecessor" in which he wrote that "the relationship between Mr. Roosevelt and myself has been one of close and sweet intimacy. It has never been ruffled in the slightest degree."[91] It wasn't until August 1910, almost two years after Taft had penned the letter, that he would finally concede that "something offended him [Roosevelt] in that letter." The combination of Taft's unfortunate insensitivity and Roosevelt's supersized ego added to the growing rift between them.

While Roosevelt's thin-skinned response to Taft's ill-mannered letter may have been the initial event in the growing deterioration of the relationship, it was not the only issue. From Roosevelt's perspective, "The break in our relations was due to no one thing, but to the cumulative effect of many things – the abandonment of everything my Administration had stood for, and other things. Taft changed greatly between the time he was elected and the time he took office."[92]

What had changed about Taft was that he was no longer just in Roosevelt's shadow, quietly and efficiently administering the affairs of the administration. He was now a power in his own right. While working for Roosevelt, he had faithfully implemented the president's policies. Now, it was his turn to develop the policies, and he turned out to be more conservative than the progressive Rough Rider thought he would be.

As Taft began to come into his own political independence, Roosevelt grew increasingly uneasy, sensing that perhaps he had picked the wrong man for the presidency. While during the campaign, Roosevelt had predicted that Taft would rank as one of the greatest presidents along with Washington and Lincoln, by the time he left for his African safari shortly after the inauguration, he had changed his opinion of the new president's chances of success: "He means well and he'll do his best. But he's weak. They'll get him. They'll lean on him."[93]

If Roosevelt had doubts about how Taft would perform as president, Taft himself also struggled to emerge from Roosevelt's long shadow. The unassuming new president had trouble thinking of himself as president. In response to being addressed as "Mr. President," Taft would look around, expecting Roosevelt to suddenly appear.[94] "I want you to know," Taft wrote to the ex-president on his safari, "that I do nothing in my work in the Executive office without considering what you would do [first]...and without having...a mental talk with you."[95]

Despite such mental talks with TR, Taft ended up making a number of decisions that were sources of irritation to Roosevelt. They were decisions that were well within the new president's right to make, but they were different from what Roosevelt would have done. Taft was not a Roosevelt clone after all. The president replaced five cabinet members that Roosevelt had appointed, decisions that TR interpreted as a personal affront to his leadership.[96] More painfully, the president fired chief forester Gifford Pinchot, a close conservation ally and personal friend of Roosevelt's.[97] TR also viewed Taft's prosecution to break up the U.S. Steel Corporation as a repudiation of actions that Roosevelt had taken as president. In Roosevelt's mind, this wasn't how Taft's presidency was supposed to have played out. Roosevelt had envisioned that the ever-loyal lieutenant would act in the same manner as he would have. He had sold the country on Taft as his successor based on this belief.

Less than a month after Taft's inauguration, the former president left for a fifteen-month African safari. He had clear misgivings about his successor, but as he noted in a May 1910 letter to his friend Henry Cabot Lodge, "for a year after Taft took office…I would not let myself think ill of anything he did." [98] TR confessed to Lodge that "I finally had to admit that he [Taft] had gone wrong on certain points."[99]

Taft was aware of his increasingly delicate relationship with the ex-president and sought to ensure that his actions and attitudes toward Roosevelt would be above reproach. He wrote to his brother, Charles that:

> I am determined if…a rupture is ever to be brought about that it shall not be brought through any action of mine. Theodore may not approve of all that I have done and I don't expect him to do so, but I shall try not to do anything which he might regard as a challenge.[100]

As Roosevelt prepared to return from his safari, Taft was concerned he would end up on the wrong end of public opinion. He knew some of his presidential decisions had displeased Roosevelt, and he worried that with TR back in the country, criticisms of his administration were sure to become more public and pronounced. To head off some of the tensions, Taft candidly admitted that his presidency hadn't turned out as he had hoped, writing to his ex-boss on May 26, 1910:

> I do not know that I have had harder luck than other Presidents but I do know that thus far I have succeeded far less than have others. I have been conscientiously trying to carry out your policies but my method of doing so has not worked smoothly.[101]

This was followed by the president's invitation for Roosevelt to visit Taft in the White House – a reunion in recognition of their years of friendship and working together, and a chance to clear the air between them. Roosevelt matter-of-factly turned him down, not wanting to lend his weight or any sign of support to Taft's failing presidency stating that "I don't think it well for an ex-president to go to the White House, or indeed to go to Washington, except when he cannot help it."[102] Taft felt his fading friend had just slapped him in the face.

When Roosevelt's ship sailed into New York City on June 18, 1910, a half million cheering people greeted him with a hero's welcome. Grinning from ear-to-ear during the ticker-tape parade that followed, TR's already enlarged ego swelled to monumental proportions. The president was conspicuously absent from the festivities, not wanting to hopelessly compete for the adoration of the crowds against the larger-than-life African adventurer.

The tension between the two titans continued to mount, with both wondering when it would all spill out into the public arena. "His whole attitude to me since his return has been unfriendly," the vexed Taft complained. "I hate to be at odds with…Roosevelt, who made me President…But, of course…I have to be President."[103]

Over time, Roosevelt's impressions and understanding of Taft had morphed. Early on he had idolized Taft as the next incarnation of Washington and Lincoln, an opinion that shifted shortly after Taft's election when he sensed that Taft would be a weak president. Now, with the distance of time and his African adventure behind him, Roosevelt was developing a more realistic and accurate understanding of his longtime friend. Taft, he realized, excelled best in situations where he was a lieutenant under a strong captain, but foundered when called upon to be his own captain. Home for just ten days, Roosevelt confided to his friend, Gifford Pinchot, who Taft had fired as chief forester:

> I keenly share your disappointment in Taft, and in a way even more deeply than you do, because it was I who made him President… My judgment is that in all probability Taft has passed his nadir. He is evidently a man who takes color from his surroundings. He was an excellent man under me, and close to me. For eighteen months after his election he was a rather pitiful failure, because he had no real strong man on whom to lean, and yielded to the advice of his

wife, his brother Charley, the different corporation lawyers who had his ear, and various similar men.[104]

Although Roosevelt had turned down the invitation to visit the White House, at the end of June he dropped in on the president at Taft's summer home in Beverly, Massachusetts. The two had not seen each other since Taft's inauguration, some sixteen months earlier. In the intervening months, Taft had bemoaned his lack of success as president, while Roosevelt critically eyed the president's dismal performance from a distance. Both men intuitively sensed the friction in the relationship, but on the surface at least, the visit was cordial.

As the president lumbered out of the house from his library where he had been reading his mail, he held out both hands in greeting to his former boss. It was an awkward moment, not just because of the mounting tensions between them, but because they were breaking new ground in presidential protocol. Here they were – a president and former president, who had at one time been best friends and close colleagues – now seeing one another for the first time since the inaugural transfer of power. How should they address one another? By first name? Should each of them be "Mr. President"?

"Ah, Theodore, it is good to see you," exclaimed Taft.

"How are you, Mr. President? This is simply bully," the former president characteristically replied.

"See here now, drop the 'Mr. President,'" said Taft, who still had trouble imagining himself as president.

"Not at all. You must be Mr. President and I am Theodore. It must be that way," Roosevelt respectfully announced.

During most of the meeting, however, Taft had trouble abiding by Roosevelt's idea of protocol and continued to address him as "Mr. President." It was a civil get-together that went better than expected. They talked about New York politics, ostensibly the purpose of the meeting, and Roosevelt entertained the president and others present with stories from his African and European excursions. At the end of two and a half hours, both men agreed that it had been a delightful reunion. "This has taken me back to some of those dear old afternoons when I was Will and you were Mr. President," Taft wistfully told his visitor.[105]

The civility of the meeting masked the growing discord between them. Although their friendship reached back two decades, their conversation had politely avoided any candid talk of the brewing storm they both knew was on the horizon. Their silence and failure to confront the real issues tragically set the stage for further deterioration of the once warm friendship.

A month and a half after the Massachusetts meeting, the president confessed to his top aide that he was "deeply wounded" and baffled by his unraveling relationship with Roosevelt:

> I am deeply hurt by his attitude and have been. If he was hurt with me, the proper thing for him to have done was to give me the opportunity to explain my position and to thrash it out as we had done many times in the past. He has closed my mouth by his seeming indifference to my administration, and it is inconceivable that I, the president of the United States, should go to him on my knees, so to speak, and ask his approval…If I only knew what the president wanted, I would do it, but you know he has held himself so aloof that I am absolutely in the dark. I am deeply wounded, and he gives me no chance to explain my attitude or learn his.[106]

In late summer, the still wildly popular ex-president embarked on a campaign-style trip out west in which he spoke to thousands of enthusiastic supporters. During the first week of September, Roosevelt and Taft were both in St. Paul for the same convention but didn't actually meet – after the president vetoed the idea of a dinner to honor both of them.[107] By and large, Roosevelt held his tongue before the crowds and was not publicly critical of the president. In fact, Taft complained privately that "in most of these speeches he has utterly ignored me."[108]

What graveled Taft more than being ignored was being upstaged. As Roosevelt stumped around the country, he exuded an almost presidential presence, choosing to momentarily fantasize that he had not given up the reins of power. Taft noted that Roosevelt "allows himself to fall into a style that makes one think he considers himself still the president of the United States."[109] The president was partially right. Roosevelt was painfully aware he wasn't president, but he still longed to return to that starring role – one that had been so natural and satisfying for him. With his still boundless energy and supersized ego, Roosevelt was grappling with what to do with the rest of his life.

TR was still young – in his early 50s and had already reached the pinnacle of success and power. He now longed for an encore. And the only appropriate second act for an ex-president would be a grand entrance back on the main stage – as president again. Roosevelt began to maneuver himself slowly and cautiously into a position that would allow him to break his fateful promise to serve only two terms. The key to freeing him to run again was if a groundswell of support from the people demanded his return – determined to divorce themselves from their disappointments with the Taft administration.

Taft instinctively knew this was Roosevelt's plan. The president gruesomely confided his fears in September, suspecting that "if you were to remove Roosevelt's skull now, you would find written on his brain '1912.'"[110]

Energized by the response he received from his swing through the west, Roosevelt couldn't help but realize that Taft had none of his charisma or leadership, something that should have been obvious to him years ago. Out of power now, TR compared himself with the president, and was coming to the painful conclusion that he had made a mistake by anointing Taft as his successor. "I think he is a better President than McKinley and probably than Harrison, but the times are totally different, and he has not the qualities that are needed at the moment."[111]

They saw each other again on September 19, 1910, at a Yale University luncheon. At Roosevelt's suggestion, they met privately afterwards to talk. It was cordial but superficial. "Roosevelt was very pleasant, and I hope that I was," Taft reported to his wife.[112] Unfortunately, they failed to candidly address their political differences – differences that were on the verge of becoming personal. Roosevelt was more interested in self-promotion than in the relationship, while Taft, who had never wanted the presidency in the first place, valued his friendship with Roosevelt more. "I shall always be grateful for what he did for me," Taft lamented, "but since he has come back [from Africa] he has seared me to the very soul." [113]

In November, Roosevelt crystallized his emerging assessment of Taft. He was unhappy with the president because Taft was simply in the wrong job. Taft's personality and style wasn't a good fit for the demands of the presidency. It was a bitter pill for Roosevelt to swallow. He had staked his reputation on Taft as his successor, but Taft had not lived up to his expectations. Taft had been "a good lieutenant, but is a poor captain,"[114] the ex-president concluded. His primary weakness was that he was "too easily influenced by the men around him," and did "not really grasp progressive principles."[115]

There was one other unspoken concern that Roosevelt had about his successor. He didn't see himself reflected in Taft's actions, and perhaps more importantly, he didn't see himself reflected at all in the new presidential mirror. Taft was certainly no Roosevelt clone – never had been, and never would be. Roosevelt had blithely expected a puppet presidency where everyone would know that he was still the power behind the throne, controlling the strings of an obedient Taft who would continue to operate unobtrusively on the sidelines. In retrospect, it is doubtful whether any successor to Theodore Roosevelt would have met his expectations. The heart of Roosevelt's discontent with the 27th president had less to do with Taft's personality or performance and more to do with TR's craving to be back in the limelight and at the center of the power he missed so much.

Despite Roosevelt's criticisms of the president, he personally liked Taft, noting that he was "a well-meaning, good-natured man, but not a leader."[116] He was "an admirable fellow." The praise was mixed with a stinging bite that foreshadowed some of what would later spew forth from TR's volcanic vocabulary. Taft was "an utterly commonplace leader; good-natured, feebly well-meaning, but with plenty of small motive; and totally unable to grasp or put into execution any great policy."[117]

A week before Thanksgiving 1910, Roosevelt returned to Washington to educate and entertain members of the National Geographic Society about his African safari. Simply being back in the capital stirred up memories of the enjoyable years he had spent as president. And with the president and his wife both out of town on separate trips, TR couldn't resist the temptation to sneak in a visit to his old house at 1600 Pennsylvania Avenue.

He had turned down Taft's earlier invitations for a White House visit. It would have been simply too painful for TR to see Taft in the seat of power that had once been his. Plus, Roosevelt didn't really want to face the awkwardness of a conversation with the man he had recently been criticizing as a weak leader.

However, with the president away on a southern states trip, Roosevelt was as eager as a boy and as confident as a king to drop by the executive mansion. He warmly greeted the workers by name, and even audaciously sat at the president's desk in the Oval Office, remembering how much he had enjoyed the presidency. Perhaps he allowed himself a moment to fantasize about reclaiming the White House.[118]

Aware of his own deficiencies as president and perhaps hoping to blunt TR's increasing criticism of him, Taft solicited Roosevelt's input in early 1911 on the president's annual message to Congress. Roosevelt must have been gratified to be consulted.[119] In March, the ever-pugnacious Roosevelt, aware of brewing problems with Mexico, asked the president for a military role if war should come. Taft agreed, subject to approval by Congress. Roosevelt was annoyed when Taft ignored his suggestion to send him to Mexico to help reconcile differences.[120]

Roosevelt's politicking and speeches continued to drive a steady wedge between him and the president. Taft found Roosevelt's actions very painful and unfair. "I confess it wounds me very deeply," Taft admitted. "I hardly think the prophet of the square deal is playing it exactly square with me now."[121] And the president was baffled, not understanding what he had done to cause such rapid deterioration of the friendship he valued so much.

> I don't see what I could have done to make things different. Somehow people have convinced the colonel that I have gone back on him, and he does not seem to be able to get that out of his mind. But it distresses me very deeply, more deeply than anyone can know, to think of him sitting there at Oyster Bay alone and feeling himself deserted.[122]

Taft's distress over the deteriorating relationship began to affect his health. He had trouble sleeping at night but would fall asleep at inappropriate times during the day. Always a big eater, he turned to food to comfort him from the stress. His weight continued to rise. "I may have been tactless," Taft finally realized, "but not intentionally did I do anything to displease him. I owe him everything. He is responsible for my being president. I am so disturbed it keeps me awake nights."[123]

Taft's big heart was no match for Roosevelt's even bigger ego that craved attention at any price. With the 1912 election looming, it was clear that Roosevelt had been infected again with the presidential bug. In the summer of 1911, the relationship between the president and ex-president continued spiraling downward as Roosevelt ratcheted up the rhetoric several notches. His language and tone became more strident as he crossed the line of civility. He began to personally insult the president, calling him a "flub-dub with a streak of the second-rate and the common in him."[124]

Roosevelt's not-so-subtle strategy was to tear down the president's reputation, while at the same time casting himself as the only man who could effectively lead America. TR's opinion of Taft had rapidly changed over the course of just a few years. Initially, Roosevelt expected Taft would be the next incarnation of Washington and Lincoln combined. That enthusiasm had been tempered by the acknowledgment that Taft wasn't a strong leader but was a good man. Finally, TR began to attack Taft personally as any support he once had for the president began to evaporate. In late October 1911, Roosevelt's opinions had hardened and there was no turning back. "As for my ever having any enthusiasm for Taft again," TR declared, "it is utterly impossible."[125]

As 1911 came to a close, Roosevelt accused Taft of being a weak leader, without clear opinions of his own, easily influenced by others, and a flip-flopper on the issues. However, he grudgingly acknowledged that Taft's intentions were probably good:

> I am really sorry for Taft. I am sure he means well, but he means well feebly, and he does not know how! He is utterly unfit for leadership, and this is a time when we need leadership. All kinds of people influence him on the unimportant things where he does know his own mind but generally makes up his mind wrong; and on the important things he does not know his own mind and changes it every which way.[126]

Roosevelt's frustration with the president stemmed only partially from his disillusionment with Taft's performance, and perhaps more with TR's own restlessness at being relegated to the sidelines of political action. The more Roosevelt criticized Taft, the more he hoped he would emerge as the logical alternative to Taft's weak leadership. The ex-president boiled with exasperation on December 29, 1911, when he wrote that "Taft is utterly hopeless...he has shown himself an entirely unfit President."[127] Furthermore, Roosevelt creatively spluttered, Taft was a "flubdub," "puzzle-witted," and a "floppy-souled creature."[128]

Taft was "deeply hurt"[129] by Roosevelt's criticism, and troubled by the rapidly disintegrating relationship. Roosevelt was his longtime friend and mentor. And Taft had tried his best to do a good job as president. On the last day of the year, Taft sadly observed that "it is hard, very hard, to see a devoted friendship going to pieces like a rope of sand."[130] Taft fatalistically acknowledged that it was very likely that Roosevelt would challenge him for the nomination, but accurately predicted that he would beat back the challenge from the Rough Rider.

Bitter Rivals

(1912)

In 1912, the gloves came off – reluctantly for Taft – as the two men slugged it out for the Republican nomination for president. Quite apart from Roosevelt's personal attacks on him, the conservative president was becoming alarmed at some of Roosevelt's radical ideas. "I believe I represent a safer and saner view of our government and its Constitution than does Theodore Roosevelt," Taft wrote to a friend in January.[131]

On Lincoln's birthday, Taft delivered a speech that was widely viewed as an attack on Roosevelt. In it, he criticized those who espoused certain views about populist government. "Such extremists are not progressives – they are political emotionalists or neurotics."[132] These were strong words for the affable Taft who still longed to be friends with Roosevelt, but who saw it as his duty to guard against what he saw as TR's extremism.

On February 21, Roosevelt finally did what Taft and many others had been predicting ever since TR returned from Africa. He announced that he was openly challenging the president for the Republican nomination. "My hat is in the ring," he roared. With his declaration, he threw aside his commitment to the "wise custom which limits the President to two terms,"[133] – words he regretted having ever escaped from his lips on election night in 1904. "I would cut that hand off there," Roosevelt grimaced pointing to his wrist, "if I could have recalled that statement."[134]

Roosevelt coveted a return to the presidency, but Taft had never really wanted the job in the first place. TR had immensely enjoyed his "bully" time being president, while Taft complained that "this is the loneliest place in the world."[135] Now that an increasingly radical Roosevelt was challenging him, Taft felt he had no honorable choice other than to fight vigorously for a second term. "Whether I win or lose is not important, but I am in this fight to perform a great public duty - the duty of keeping Theodore Roosevelt out of the White House."[136]

Taft didn't like conflict but went on the offensive in late April. He warned a large crowd in Boston that Roosevelt was a threat to the nation since he was positioning himself to serve as president for life. "There is not the slightest reason why," Taft predicted, "if he secures a third term, and the limitation of the Washington, Jefferson and Jackson tradition is broken down, he should not have as many terms as his natural life will permit. If he is necessary now to the government, why not later?"[137] It was a tough speech for the good-natured president to deliver.

After the speech, a newspaper reporter found a despondent president hunched over in his railroad car. Taft was visibly shaken and sighed deeply, "Roosevelt was my closest friend."[138] Overcome by emotions, the president then broke into tears.

The very public campaign for the nomination quickly turned personal as both Taft and Roosevelt escalated their language and resorted to name calling. Taft was a "fathead"[139] and had the "brains of a guinea pig," according to Roosevelt.[140]

Roosevelt's ruthless drive for the presidency led Taft to conclude that Roosevelt was "beside himself with rage."[141] Having now made an open break with the president, Roosevelt's ego, as well as his honor, were on the line, and his actions were increasingly aggressive. "The conduct of the colonel is certainly that of a desperate man who stops at nothing," Taft noted fearfully.[142]

Taft was in a fight he didn't want with a friend he didn't want to lose. As he campaigned, he would say to his audience:

This wrenches my soul. I am here to reply to an old and true friend of mine, Theodore Roosevelt, who has made many charges against me. I deny those charges. I deny all of them. I do not want to fight Theodore Roosevelt, but sometimes a man in a corner fights. I am going to fight.[143]

Difficult as it was for the amiable Taft, he began to lash back at Roosevelt as they battled for the heart of the Republican party and the nomination. He accused Roosevelt of being a "dangerous demagogue,"[144] a "dangerous egotist,"[145] a "flatterer of the people,"[146] and a "honey-fugler" (which was then a common mid-western term meaning mealy-mouthed wheedler).[147]

As the nomination battle intensified, Roosevelt shot back that Taft was "boss-controlled," and a "standpatter."[148]

In June, Taft – still in charge of the party's machine – narrowly beat back the challenge of the former president. The victory, however, was shrouded in controversy over disputed delegates that had been assigned almost universally to Taft. After the convention, there was talk of getting the two combatants to meet and resolve their differences. Roosevelt indigently snuffed out the possibility of any such meeting: "I hold that Mr. Taft stole the nomination, and I do not feel like arbitrating with a pickpocket as to whether or not he shall keep my watch."[149]

Taft was relieved and satisfied with his victory: "Whatever happens in November, we have achieved the most important end and that is that Roosevelt can not be President."[150] However, that was before Roosevelt bolted from the Republican Party and launched his own Progressive Party (Bull Moose) ticket in August, setting the stage for more mudslinging in a bitter three-way race between Roosevelt, Taft, and New Jersey Governor Woodrow Wilson.

With the threat of a third term once again a possibility, Taft went on the offensive with increasingly slanderous accusations. He charged that Roosevelt was "the most dangerous man that we have had in this country since its origin,"[151] a "megalomaniac."[152] "He is to be classed with the leaders of religious cults. I look upon him as I look upon a freak, almost."[153]

Privately to his wife, Taft described Roosevelt as the

> fakir, the juggler, the green-goods man, the gold brick man that he
> has come to be...I have not any feeling of enmity against Roosevelt

or any feeling of hatred. I look upon him as an historical character of a most peculiar type...[154]

Not to be outdone by his friend turned nemesis, Roosevelt labeled Taft as "a serpent's tooth."[155] Once during the campaign when Roosevelt was asked about Taft, he bit his tongue and held back from further invective, saying only that "I never discuss dead issues."[156]

The incendiary campaign rhetoric between these two former friends became such a bitter battle that Taft peevishly and spitefully confided to his wife that "if I can not win, I hope Wilson will, and Roosevelt feels that if he can not win, he hopes Wilson will."[157] They both got their second wish. As the election returns poured in from across the nation that November, Wilson won a resounding victory in the Electoral College: 435 votes, to Roosevelt's 88, with an embarrassingly meager 8 votes for the sitting president.

Reconciliation

(1913 – 1919)

While the acrimonious fight between Roosevelt and Taft was intensely personal – with mean-spirited name calling on both sides – the disintegration of their friendship in 1912 was never really driven by personal issues between the two men. In retrospect, it was Roosevelt who picked the fight. He was obsessed with himself and with power. And he was at sea with an identity crisis after he relinquished the presidency to Taft in March 1909. Taft understood that this is what drove Roosevelt to become "temperamentally irresponsible."[158]

Roosevelt's poor judgment (or wishful thinking) had also misled him into thinking that Taft would be an outstanding president – a mirror image of Roosevelt and competition for greatness with Washington and Lincoln. Nothing could have been further from the truth. Taft had a judicial mindset, not a charismatic leadership persona so important for the presidency

– especially after the example that TR had set. Taft disliked the roughness of politics. Had Taft had his way, absent the wily influence of his wife and her leaning on Roosevelt, he would never have run for the presidency in the first place.

When Roosevelt found himself sidelined from political action in early 1909 and observed Taft's ineptitude in pulling the strings of the presidency as he had done, he became agitated. All it took was one imagined affront – equating Taft's brother, Charley, with Roosevelt as being responsible for Taft's election – to give Roosevelt the excuse he needed to enter the arena once again.

With Woodrow Wilson in the White House, Roosevelt and Taft were no longer fierce competitors, and time began to slowly work its healing power to bring about a limited reconciliation between them. It was not until April 1915 that circumstances brought them together again for an awkward first encounter.

The occasion was a sad one – the funeral of a Yale professor they had both known. Knowing that Roosevelt would also be there, Taft imagined what seeing TR again would be like. He took the high road in a letter to a friend: "I don't know how he will conduct himself, but I shall try to be pleasant." Taft continued, reflecting a deep understanding of human nature and how TR had wounded him, that "it is the man who has done the wrong who finds it difficult to forgive the man whom he has treated badly."[159]

Taft kept his eye out for Roosevelt at the funeral. When he caught sight of him, he maturely took the initiative. He walked up to him, put out his hand and warmly addressed the former president as only a very close friend could – ignoring TR's previous titles of "president" and "colonel." "How are you, Theodore?"

Roosevelt was taken by surprise and hadn't recognized his successor until he greeted him. It was the start of a slow healing in the relationship – "a bit stiff," Taft noted later, "but it was all right." The stiffness was to be expected given what they had been through. "It was pleasant enough, but it was not cordial or intimate," Taft continued.[160]

In 1916, the two former presidents saw each other again at a meeting in New York City – but not surprisingly a genuine reconciliation remained elusive. The civil meeting did serve a purpose, however, in helping to correct the speculation of the press about the relationship. Taft noted that the press "had given the impression that if Roosevelt and I met, he would curse me and I would curse him, and each would kick the other in the stomach."[161]

The days of cursing and kicking in the relationship were fading, even though Taft, not surprisingly, still harbored some resentment toward Roosevelt. When told that Roosevelt would be campaigning in the west for Charles Evans Hughes, Taft was relieved: "The farther he goes away the better."[162]

Despite Taft's occasional irritation, he was realizing that life is too short "to maintain these quarrels no matter what the justice of them."[163] From Taft's perspective, he had been clearly wronged. Writing to his son, Charlie, on March 16, 1918, Taft recalled that

> Roosevelt did me a great injury and great injustice, but he did himself more…I cherish no resentment against Roosevelt because such attitude of mind is not congenial to me. It only worries the resenter and works little harm to the resentee. If opportunity came to get even, I would feel myself above it…I am glad to be on good terms with a man for many of whose traits and abilities I have great admiration, to whom I am indebted for many generous acts, and many great opportunities.[164]

Two incidents that year also reminded Roosevelt that life is short and that his own clock was ticking away. He appeared to soften some.

In February, he was hospitalized for abscesses in his leg and thigh, ended up having an emergency operation, and stayed in the hospital for a month. He was becoming a frail man. A sympathy telegram from Taft opened a door for further reconciliation.

Then a few months later in July, Roosevelt was struck with deep grief upon learning of the death of his son, Quentin, in the war in Europe. Taft again reached out to his former friend, telegraphing his words of condolence. "His was a noble life gloriously ended," wrote Taft. "Our sympathy for you is deeper when we remember that Quentin and Charlie were boys together and babes in the same year."[165]

In addition to the reminders of their own humanity, their combined opposition to President Wilson's policies opened the way for a limited reconciliation. Politics had driven them apart, but it now brought them together. After the rancor of 1912, Wilson was "chief bond between us," Taft noted.[166]

Taft was delighted when Roosevelt sent him one of his speeches and asked for Taft's advice, some of which he took.[167] In May 1918, the two ex-presidents both found themselves at the same hotel in Chicago, and Taft reached out to greet his former boss in the dining room of the Blackstone Hotel. They spent a warm and cordial half hour together.[168] Concerned about the direction of the country under Wilson, they both campaigned that fall to help elect a Republican Congress.

It was the Rough Rider's last campaign. On January 5, 1919, his body worn out, Theodore Roosevelt quietly passed away in his sleep. The nation was shocked and mourned, but TR's death was particularly painful for Taft.

At Roosevelt's graveside burial, with snow covering the ground, Taft wept. Roosevelt had been one of his first friends in Washington, and for years had been his closest friend. Three times President Roosevelt had offered him a seat on the Supreme Court. He had appointed him secretary of war and later anointed him as president. And then they had become bitter rivals in 1912 as Roosevelt sought to reclaim the presidency. In the last few years, they had made peace with one another.

"I want to say," Taft wrote a friend, "how glad I am Theodore and I came together after that long painful interval. Had he died in a hostile state of mind toward me, I would have mourned the fact all my life. I loved him always and cherish his memory."[169]

Even in later years, as the two men united in their opposition to Woodrow Wilson and reached a limited reconciliation, their relationship was never again the same as it had been in the early years of the friendship.

Theirs was a warm friendship and sad rivalry that shaped the landscape of the nation and the world. Through it all, Taft had the bigger heart and Roosevelt the bigger ego. While Taft maligned Roosevelt with his own share of choice zingers, he did so reluctantly and only after Roosevelt had gone on the offensive and begun to sputter invective against his former colleague. Taft had never wanted to fight with his friend, and never really understood why he was being unjustly attacked. Roosevelt had created the feud of 1912 because of his frustration with not being the center of attention – with not being president. With a monumental ego, it was therefore easy for him to elevate himself by finding fault with his successor.

For a quarter century, their genial friendship and close political partnership significantly impacted each of their careers and national politics. It is unlikely either man would have become president without the supportive friendship they enjoyed. Roosevelt made Taft president and without their friendship, Taft would have never become president. Roosevelt's career would have never taken off without Taft's help in landing the important assistant secretary of the Navy position.

Unfortunately, their friendship tragically imploded and splintered to produce one of the most bitter political feuds ever witnessed in American history. Their friendship and later fight in the 1912 presidential election changed the course of history.

MASTER AND PUP

Franklin D. Roosevelt and Lyndon B. Johnson

Dreamers

(Early Years)

E ven as a young boy, Lyndon Baines Johnson was driven to dominate people and shape events. He was driven by an unshakeable and deep craving to be somebody, to make something of his life, to be noticed, to be important, – to be respected. He was genetically incapable of sitting patiently on the sidelines and waiting for things to happen or emerge. He found he loved amassing and wielding power. Lofty daydreams about his future consumed his thinking, while he fought off nightmares of growing old and forever trapped in the Hill Country of Texas, often waking in a sweat as he repeated to himself, "I must get away. I must get away."[170]

At each stage of his life, he carefully mapped out what was necessary to have the daydreams prevail over the nightmares. As a young adolescent, he once blurted out in all seriousness to some startled schoolmates, "Someday I'm going to be President of the United States."[171] For his friends, it was a totally out of context outburst, and they laughed at him. For Lyndon, it was simply the expression of a grand vision that was taking shape in his mind and tugging at his heart, as he plotted his escape from the hardscrabble poverty of central Texas. More importantly, he was driven to achieve so he would not end up penniless and humiliated like his father. The ridicule of his classmates of his presidential ambitions probably only strengthened his resolve.

With a colossal ego and larger-than-life presence, Lyndon had a natural ability to maneuver, finagle, and inject himself into the middle of anything and everything. He loved being the center of attention. To reach his goals, he was quite willing to let personal ethics ride in the back seat, or perhaps more appropriately, to be locked in the trunk. He wouldn't allow anything to stand in his way.

In the closing days of 1931, the gangly 23-year-old Johnson, for all his swagger and confidence and dreams, found himself temporarily like a fish out of water. As close to a Texas hillbilly as you can get, he had just stepped off the train in Washington, D.C. for the first time. The nation's capital, with the splendor of its architecture and the smell of importance and power in the air, was like a different planet for Lyndon. It was far removed from the small-town insignificance and dust of Johnson City, Texas.

Yet here he was, ignorant and unsophisticated, ready to start his duties as secretary to a newly elected congressman, Richard Kleberg from the 14th District in Texas. Johnson knew nothing – nothing about how things worked in Washington, how to do his job, or even how to open a bank account in which to deposit his first paycheck.[172]

Those early days in Washington must have been unsettling ones for the power and control driven Johnson as he grappled with how to find his way in a brand-new city and amongst unknown power brokers – and most importantly for him, with how to find or create a power vacuum in which he could become somebody other than a lowly secretary to a freshman congressman.

Lyndon Johnson's arrival in Washington coincided with the winter of the nation's Depression as the hapless administration of President Herbert Hoover continued to disintegrate, and as more and more Americans lost their jobs. For all of his administrative reputation and skills, Hoover had drawn a constitutional line in the sand, arguing that he did not have the power as president to take more aggressive action to combat the nation's economic woes. The fact that the charismatically challenged Hoover exuded dourness and dryness certainly didn't help inspire the nation's confidence.

The unnaturally self-confident Johnson certainly wouldn't have had any compunction about exercising whatever power was necessary – whether constitutional or not – and neither, for that matter would Hoover's successor Franklin D. Roosevelt.

Less than a month after Johnson's arrival in Washington, his new boss gave Lyndon and another assistant two complimentary tickets to hear Hoover speak to a joint session of Congress on the economic crisis and his proposals to "unshackle the forces of recovery."[173] However, when Johnson and Estelle Harbin arrived at the House gallery on January 4, 1932, their hearts sank with disappointment as they surveyed the scene. The gallery was packed, and they realized they hadn't come early enough. With no seats left, they camped out instead, sitting "on the top two steps." Miss Harbin later recalled that "Lyndon was there beside me as scared as I was. We sat there like two scared field mice."[174]

However, something besides fear was also stirring in Johnson. He had never before been in such a grand setting with so many powerful people. It was the first time he had ever been that close to a president. And so, despite knowing that he was just a bit player in this unfolding drama before him and feeling that he was out of his comfort zone, he was keenly observing everything before him – soaking in like a sponge all the details and making mental notes about this somber and power-packed occasion.

He learned fast. Miss Harbin noted that "he couldn't stand not being somebody – just could not stand it. So he was trying to meet everyone, to learn everything – he was trying to gobble up all Washington in a month."[175] And by all accounts, he did a pretty good job at it. Another congressional secretary who knew Johnson then noted that "this skinny boy was as green as anybody could be, but within a few months he knew how to operate in Washington better than some who had been here twenty years."[176]

In learning the politics of the capitol, he began to accumulate and wield power – he was becoming somebody. After being on the job just over a year, he manipulated an election that gave him a power base as Speaker of The Little Congress, a stagnant old-timers organization of congressional aides. He took over the group and quickly revitalized it. Using his speakership, he met and rubbed shoulders with influential people he invited to address the group. He also acted as a surrogate congressman for his absentee boss, who found he preferred hitting the golf links and attending parties to the congressional work, allowing Johnson to act in his stead – even impersonating him at times on the phone.

Johnson didn't just remain anonymous and in the background – that wasn't his style. He was the ultimate self-promoter and networker. He began to build his own personal brand and take credit for everything the congressman's office did. He made sure that the name "Lyndon B. Johnson" was prominently plastered in news releases and letters as he interacted with constituents, federal agencies, members of Congress, and congressional staff. He wanted people to know that he was the real power behind the throne – as in fact he really was in this case.

For a boy who had long dreamed of becoming president one day, there could be nothing more exhilarating than to stand in the cold damp air of Washington and personally witness the transfer of presidential power. It was March 4, 1933, and Johnson – not yet 25-years-old – was one of many hopeful faces in a vast sea of humanity that stood facing the East Front of the Capitol to witness Franklin Roosevelt's inauguration as president.[177]

For Roosevelt, the day marked the fulfillment of his dreams – the crowning climax of a political blueprint he had drawn for himself. Like Johnson, Roosevelt had early dreams of becoming President. He had often envisioned himself following in the footsteps of his famous cousin, Theodore, and at major steps of his career, he had imitated the Rough Rider's rise to power. Unlike Johnson, whose family name was only associated with the inconsequential and desolate settlement of Johnson City (population less than 500), Roosevelt was heir to the country's most famous political name. Roosevelt's early hope of eventually landing in the White House had been plausible. From the New York State legislature, to Assistant Secretary of the Navy, to Governor of New York, he seemed to be on the presidential track that Theodore had traveled.

Johnson's embryonic and quixotic dreams were stacked against him, and he would have to work hard to build a name for himself since he hadn't been fortunate enough to inherit one that everyone recognized. As Johnson stood in the crowd watching history being made in front of his eyes, he soaked in all the details of the moment, imagining what it would be like for him to be at the rostrum one day taking the presidential oath of office. His reverie was broken by the intruding noise and jostling of those around him. Today he was just a nameless face in the crowd, but he so desperately wanted to be somebody – to stand out and be in charge.

With banks failing at an alarming rate, Johnson heard the new President somberly assert to the troubled nation his "firm belief that the only thing we have to fear is fear itself." Johnson admired Roosevelt's self-confidence in confronting the biggest crisis since the Civil War. The President didn't seem afraid of anything. "He was," Johnson later noted after FDR's death, "the one person I ever knew, anywhere, who was never afraid."[178] He might have been surprised to learn that Roosevelt had confessed to his son, James, on the night of his election as President that "I'm just afraid that I may not have the strength to do the job."[179] Nevertheless, on inauguration day and throughout the twelve years he would eventually serve as president, Roosevelt exuded confidence, just as Johnson's self-confidence seemed to know no bounds.

For the next few years, Johnson continued to amass power – power well beyond what a congressional secretary would normally have. He met the right people on Capitol Hill and in the federal bureaucracy. He brazenly ingratiated himself to them. He became a "professional son' to many older and influential men. He quickly gained a reputation as someone who could get things done in Washington. However, he was still only a congressional secretary and he wanted more. He was energetic and fiercely ambitious.

From a Distance

(1935 – 1937)

In the early summer of 1935, Johnson forcibly pried opened a political window to move his dreams to the next level. President Roosevelt had just announced the creation of a new agency – the National Youth Administration (NYA) that was designed to provide job training and part-time work for young people. The program in each state would be autonomously managed by a director appointed by the President. When Johnson's roommate, who was secretary to Texas Congressman Maury Maverick, told Johnson about the NYA Texas job, Johnson audaciously and confidently stated "I'd like that job."[180] It was more than an idle remark, but a decision to actively pull out all the stops to pursue this long-shot opportunity.

LBJ cajoled and pressured Maverick and another Texas congressman, the influential Sam Rayburn to lobby the President, the state's two senators, and the national NYA director on his behalf. He had charmed his way into friendships with both Maverick and Rayburn, and so they were willing to go to bat for the young congressional secretary. In addition to Lyndon reaching out to Rayburn, his relationship with the congressman had been enhanced by family connections. Rayburn and Johnson's father, Sam Johnson, had served together in the Texas Legislature, and Rayburn held a special affection in his heart for Lyndon's father and "always remembered [him] with interest and kindly feeling."[181]

Despite his earnest lobbying effort, Lyndon's appointment to the NYA job would be as difficult as pushing a twenty-pound boulder uphill, armed only with a lonely toothpick. He simply didn't have the credentials to create and run a major federal program on a statewide basis. He had three major strikes against him: First, he was only 26 years old; second, he had no significant administrative experience; and third, the president had no idea who he was. So naturally, Roosevelt was more than reluctant to risk the success of the NYA in the largest state by appointing such an unknown and untested person to manage job creation for kids just a little younger than Johnson himself. Such an appointment just didn't make practical or political sense.

Nevertheless, Rayburn, out of fondness for both Lyndon and his father, was willing to gamble whatever political influence and capital he had with the President. Rayburn, who in less than two years would be the house majority leader, convinced the White House to pencil his name in on the president's busy calendar. When he met with Roosevelt, he poured out his most persuasive arguments on why this skinny congressional secretary from one of the most isolated regions of Texas should get the job. We don't know exactly what he said, but amazingly, after Rayburn's White House meeting, an earlier announcement of the appointment of a Texas director (who had actually been sworn in too) was mysteriously rescinded as a mistake, and Johnson, against all odds, got the nod.

Roosevelt had personally intervened and just given this ambitious kid's fledgling career a very lucky break and significant boost – the first of many he would bestow on Johnson in the years ahead. A presidential appointment was heady stuff for Johnson, but he barely paused before planning what his next step would be. At a farewell party for the young congressional aide, Johnson prophetically announced, "When I come back to Washington, I'm coming back as a Congressman."[182]

He packed his belongings and moved back to Texas where he energetically threw himself into creating and running the statewide NYA organization, dominating the staff he had assembled with his often-inhuman performance expectations. The job was what he wanted – at least for now – but the job did have its drawbacks.

While in Washington, he had schmoozed with powerful members of Congress. In Texas, he was removed from the corridors of national power. He was away from the real action he lived and breathed for. However, Lyndon had the ability to create excitement and build a power base in whatever situation he found himself. He knew he had been given an incredible opportunity, and so he rolled up his sleeves to build an organization that would make the president he had still never met proud.

He did meet Eleanor Roosevelt, who came to Johnson's Austin office in 1936 to find out the secret of the Texas NYA organization's success. He shook hands with the First Lady and showed her around. His chances of actually meeting the busy president rested on slimmer hopes.

When news reached Texas that FDR would visit Dallas for the Texas Centennial Exposition in 1936, Lyndon resolved to at least be seen by the president. After learning the route of the presidential motorcade, Johnson positioned himself, along with hundreds of Texas NYA boys, by the side of the road. As the Roosevelt passed by in his car, Lyndon stood there with his boys as they saluted the president with their shovels.[183]

Managing the Texas NYA and anonymously saluting the commander-in-chief wasn't what Johnson wanted to do long-term. While it was a strategic opportunity to begin to build a statewide organization of loyal followers who would help Johnson in his later quests for elective office, he viewed it as only a temporary steppingstone. His chance to make the next step came in late February 1937. It was a big stretch that lay at the foundation of his deliberate plan that would eventually take him to the White House.

After almost a quarter century in Congress, 10th District Texas congressman James Paul Buchanan died on February 22. Johnson quickly made the decision to run in the special election to fill the vacancy. It was too good to pass up, and opportunities like this didn't come along every day. He realized it was a long-shot gamble. He would have to resign his NYA job in order to campaign full-time for the next 40 days – but it could be his ticket back to Washington.

Rumors of Johnson's plans to quit filtered up to the head of the NYA, who was alarmed at the prospect of losing him. "He's my whole youth program in Texas, and if he quits I have no program down there," lamented Administrator Aubrey Williams to the president's assistant Thomas Corcoran.

Corcoran relayed the concerns to the president. Roosevelt, who had only reluctantly appointed Johnson in the first place, and who had still never met this Texas wonder boy, was also apprehensive about the impact Johnson's resignation would have on the success of the Texas NYA. And so he directed Corcoran to contact Johnson with the president's instructions that Johnson must drop out of the congressional race and stay with the NYA.

As fate would have it, the call from the White House to Johnson on Monday, March 1 came too late. Johnson had formally resigned the day before.[184] Had the call reached Johnson before he resigned, it's doubtful that even an appeal from the president of the United States would have dissuaded him from pursuing the open House seat. It was an important step in the career he had long dreamed about. It was part of his road map to become somebody – and to have a leading and powerful role on the national stage.

Johnson was one of eight candidates vying for the vacant seat. He was not nearly as well-known as some of his rivals who had built up reputations, connections, and good will over many years. He was also just 28-years-old. Only two members of the House of Representatives were younger.[185] Funding the campaign was an immediate concern. Lots of money would be needed to pay for the short, but intense race. Johnson's wife, Lady Bird, came to the rescue by convincing her father to advance $10,000 of her inheritance. This freed Lyndon from having to spend time raising money and allowed him to work full-time actually drumming up votes.

To distinguish himself from the competition, Johnson enthusiastically hitched his wagon to President Roosevelt and his policies, including FDR's ill-fated scheme to expand the number of justices on the U.S. Supreme Court (the infamous "court-packing" plan). All eyes were on Texas as the race was widely seen as a referendum of the president and his policies.

Johnson campaigned hard and spent long days driving to cities, towns, and isolated farmhouses in the district. He was an awkward and bumbling public speaker, but when his speeches were over, he was in his element – very naturally shaking hands and hugging members of the audience. In his drive to reach every possible voter and leave no stone unturned, he was pushing himself to the point of physical exhaustion. On April 8, two days before the special election, and still frantically charging hard for the seat, Johnson collapsed in Austin. The campaign was over for him. He was rushed to the hospital for emergency removal of his appendix.

He was still sidelined, recuperating and captive to his hospital bed, as election officials reported he had won, collecting more than twice as many votes as any of his competitors. The rest of the nation, including the president, learned the same news as it was emblazoned on the front page of major newspapers across the country. Rather than immediately depart for Washington to take the oath of office, Johnson was delayed, first by his continued hospitalization, and second by an opportunity to finally meet the president in person, shake his hand, and have his picture taken with him.

Instant Rapport
(1937)

Roosevelt began a ten-day fishing vacation in the Gulf of Mexico on the first of May. The next day, Texas Governor Jimmy Allred, who happened to be a friend of Johnson, boarded the presidential yacht, the U.S.S. *Potomac*. The governor and president discussed plans for a reception for FDR in Galveston at the end of the fishing trip and arranged for a meeting with the newly elected congressman. "The President will be very happy indeed to see you when he lands at Galveston," Allred wrote Johnson. "He was intensely interested in the details of your campaign, and himself brought up the [Agriculture] committee matter which you and I discussed. I suggested to him that you all should have your picture made together next week, and this was entirely agreeable."[186] Lyndon was thrilled with the chance to finally meet his idol, on whom he had staked his campaign.

When May 11 arrived, the newly minted congressman-elect was still thin and gaunt from his weeks of hospitalization, and the toll the rigorous campaign had exacted on him. He rehearsed in his mind what the moment would be like when he greeted the president and finally shook his hand. During his lifetime, Johnson would eventually come to know at least a half-dozen presidents,[187] but this was to be his first such encounter. FDR, of course, was no stranger to presidents. It ran in the family; his distant cousin, Theodore, had been president. FDR had also worked for President Wilson as assistant secretary of the navy, serving in Wilson's war cabinet along with the administrative genius and humanitarian, Herbert Hoover.

Lyndon was dressed in a new black pin-striped, double-breasted suit he had purchased especially for the occasion. He had a white orchid in his lapel. Standing somewhat anxiously on the Galveston dock, Johnson and the crowd of dignitaries waited for the commander-in-chief. After an hour-long delay the confident and smiling Roosevelt appeared and hoisted himself down the gangplank, using his powerful hands and arms on the railings on either side to propel himself toward the waiting crowd.

"Mr. President," Governor Allred said in greeting Roosevelt, "I'd like to present our new Congressman."[188] The president and the youthful congressman-elect shook hands, with broad smiles radiating from their faces as they confidently locked eyes and sized up one another.

Roosevelt may well have thought back to his own first electoral victory in 1910 when he had been sent to the New York State Senate. Like Johnson, he had been only 28 when he was first elected – in fact, just about two months older than Johnson was on his election day. And while a generation separated the two men, they both had politics in their blood – influential relatives who began political careers even earlier. Roosevelt had been inspired by his famous cousin Theodore, who had been just 23 when he was elected to the New York State Assembly. Johnson was influenced by his father Sam, who had been elected to the Texas House of Representatives when he was 27 years old.

The photographers snapped pictures of Roosevelt and Johnson, freezing in time the historical moment when a cross generational friendship was crystallized – when the experimentation of the New Deal met the passion of the Great Society. Of course, Governor Allred was there also between the two men, but for Johnson in later campaigns, Allred's presence in the photo was an inconvenient truth and so he had the governor's image airbrushed out to show just Roosevelt and himself.

The 32nd president and the future 36th president engaged in small talk as they got acquainted with one another. Johnson was determined not to let this meeting with the President fade into just a momentary one-time handshake, and so he kept up the conversation with the master conversationalist. Like old friends, the two gregarious men talked easily and naturally about the president's successful fishing trip: he had caught two tarpon, one which weighed ninety pounds.[189] Bluffing his way into the president's good graces, Johnson told FDR that fishing was a favorite pastime of his. It was a comment "which would have surprised those who knew him,"[190] according to biographer Merle Miller.

The creative ploy worked. FDR was impressed with Lyndon. He liked this assertive young congressman-elect who had campaigned so wholeheartedly for his policies. Unfortunately, there wasn't time now to get to know him better. Others were standing around clamoring for a word, a smile, and a handshake from the president. However, FDR wasn't quite ready to end the conversation, so he invited Lyndon to join him on the presidential train that day for the 300 mile plus journey from Galveston to Fort Worth.

The train whistled past mile after mile of the Texas landscape filled with presidential well-wishers. Lyndon must have pinched himself at his good fortune to be traveling with the president of the United States. He eagerly searched for common ground and conversational topics with Roosevelt.

Then he remembered that Roosevelt had served as assistant secretary of the Navy under President Wilson, just as Theodore Roosevelt had earlier served in the same position in the McKinley administration. Pouring on the flattery, Johnson feigned that the two Roosevelts had inspired his lifelong interest in the Navy. It was another remark "that would have astonished his friends,"[191] had they been present. In Johnson's world, however, truth was less important than image and results. The conversation continued. The president liked this freshman congressman-elect and admitted to him that: "I can always use a good man to help out with naval matters in Congress."[192]

As the train neared Fort Worth and the end of Johnson's hours of a captive audience with the president, the congressman hoped that his budding relationship with Roosevelt would not simply evaporate once he stepped off the train, but that the camaraderie between the two had been mutual. If there was any question whether the president had taken a liking to this savvy boy, that doubt was erased as FDR reached for pencil and paper. He scrawled something down, and handed the slip of paper to Johnson, and said, "Here's a telephone number. When you get to Washington, call it and ask for Tom.

Tell him what we've talked about."[193] The paper contained the phone number for the president's White House assistant Thomas Corcoran.

It had been a remarkable day for Johnson – meeting, riding with, and talking one-on-one with the President of the United States. For this privilege, Lyndon had emptied his pockets of all his cash when he obediently paid the train fare demanded by the conductor. He wasn't sure he should have done that; after all, Roosevelt had invited him. A reporter told him to remember that "the president is very generous with everybody's money but his own."[194] The trip had been well worth the cost.

Back in the Oval Office and before Johnson could call Corcoran as directed, the president summoned his aide to describe his conversation with Lyndon. "I've just met the most remarkable young man," the President declared to Corcoran. "Now I like this boy, and you're going to help him with anything you can."[195]

Why did Franklin Roosevelt like Lyndon Johnson? Johnson's reputation obviously preceded him. This was the boy who Roosevelt had appointed, sight unseen, as Texas director of the NYA, and who, despite the strikes against him, had risen to the challenge. Eleanor had been impressed with him. This was the boy who had based his entire congressional campaign on complete support for the president and his policies, delivering for Roosevelt a referendum victory.

Beyond these surface issues, both men must have sensed they were almost talking to their alter ego. They were similar in many respects. Neither seemed afraid of anything. Roosevelt liked Johnson's uninhibited enthusiasm. The poor boy from the hardscrabble Hill Country of Texas had used sheer determination and hard work to rise out of poverty and get to where he was. And the patrician from the privileged life of Hyde Park, New York had also used sheer determination and hard work to not let polio defeat him. While the miles and lifestyles that separated the Hill Country from Hyde Park were vast, both men loved to exercise control and manipulate the levers of power. In addition, neither felt particularly constrained to be scrupulously honest, but felt comfortable in stretching truth to fit the occasion and the needs.

Back in Washington, Roosevelt continued to think about the lanky new Texas congressman. He shared his wistful and prophetic thoughts with his secretary of the interior, Harold Ickes who remembered the president saying that "if he hadn't gone to Harvard, that's the kind of uninhibited young pro he'd like to be – that in the next generation the balance of power would shift south and west, and this boy could well be the first Southern President."[196]

In meeting and impressing Franklin Roosevelt, Lyndon Johnson had obtained a powerful benefactor who could help to advance his fledgling congressional career. The President had decided he wanted Johnson on the House Naval Affairs Committee and so he unleashed his casual and folksy charm to make it happen. Thus, over a congenial dinner at the White House with Democratic Congressman Fred Vinson of the House Ways and Means Committee (the Democrats on the committee decided on committee assignments for freshmen Democrats in the House), the President casually suggested toward the end of the evening: "Fred, there's a fine young man just come to the House. Fred, you know that young fellow, Lyndon Johnson? I think he would be a great help on [the] Naval Affairs [Committee]."[197] Vinson got the message and Johnson got the appointment.

Obtaining Power

(1938)

However, the landlocked and arid Hill Country that Johnson represented wasn't all that interested in naval affairs and, quite frankly, neither was he. More immediate and practical matters consumed their thinking. One of Congressman Johnson's early and ambitious goals was to bring electricity to the poor and rural Hill Country. To do so required money – in the form of a federal loan from the Rural Electrification Administration (REA). In order to obtain the loan, the area needed to form an electric cooperative to manage power distribution. To form the cooperative, sufficient signatures on a petition were required. Here, Johnson faced an uphill battle.

While certain leaders in the Hill Country wanted electricity, many of the country folks were skeptical of why they needed electricity in the first place. One resident asked: "Something you had never had or experienced – are you going to miss it?"[198] They were also concerned about their ability to pay their monthly electric bill, about going into debt, and possibly losing their land. And so, the signatures on the petition fell short. Even more challenging, however, was the low population density of the Hill Country. To ensure that its loans were repaid, the REA required that there be at least three customers per mile of transmission line. The sparsely populated Hill Country fell significantly short on this count – only 1.3 people per mile.

Johnson was undeterred. He assured the local leaders he would find a way to obtain the loan. "I'll get it for you," he confidently asserted. "I'll go to the REA. I'll go to the President if I have to. But we will get the money."[199] As promised, he went to the REA, but was rebuffed by a wall of regulations, and so he used his ace in the hole – he appealed directly to the president. He obtained an appointment with FDR during the second week of June 1938. It was his first private meeting with the president since his triumphant Texas train trip over a year earlier.

Roosevelt had a well-deserved reputation for steering and dominating conversations – something for which Johnson was also known. In fact, Johnson was warned before entering the Oval Office that "When you get in there, he'll filibuster you to death. You won't get a word in."[200] According to Raymond Moley, a member of the president's brain trust and sometimes speech writer, FDR's "visitors didn't talk back to him. They couldn't. It was he who called the conversational turns, he who would discourse at length on this or that, he who would catch and hold and visibly delight the caller."[201]

As Johnson began to show the President pictures of a recently completed dam that would be the source of the power for the Hill Country, Roosevelt began the predicted filibuster: "That's a multiple-arch dam, Lyndon, and I do believe it's the largest multiple-arch dam I've ever seen."[202] The president continued waxing eloquent on multiple-arch dams. Lyndon was aware that the clock on his appointment was ticking away. He was also keenly observing the president's style and manner and picking up a few tips for later use.

In the conversational showdown of the two talkative titans, Roosevelt was clearly the master, with position, age, and experience all on his side. With other people, Johnson had no trouble dominating a conversation, using what became known as "The Johnson Treatment." Often, he would grab the lapel jacket of his intended victim, thrust his face to within inches of the other, and pour out his most persuasive arguments. Newspaper columnist Mary McGrory would later describe Johnson's style as "an incredible, potent mixture of persuasion, badgering, flattery, threats, reminders of past favors and future advantages."[203] Johnson recognized that such treatment with the president would not only be inappropriate but impractical on the man who remained seated due to his paralysis.

Finally, Johnson managed to force a word in edgewise to the presidential monologue and explained his concern: "Water, water everywhere, not a drop to drink! Power, power everywhere, but not in a home on the banks of these rural rivers!"[204] Johnson had hit a responsive chord with the president. The chance to help improve the lot of the southern poor appealed to Roosevelt.

FDR immediately picked up the phone and called the REA director, John Carmody, while Johnson listened to the president's end of the conversation. "John," Roosevelt exclaimed, "there's a young congressman in my office, Lyndon Johnson." "He's an old friend of mine,"[205] the president continued, conveniently ignoring the fact that he had known Johnson for just over a year and had had little contact with him in the intervening months. After explaining Johnson's proposal for an REA loan, he listened while Carmody described the REA's regulations and why Johnson's proposal was not in compliance with the requirements.

Regardless, the president liked Lyndon and wanted to help him, and he had the power to do so. "John," FDR said disarmingly and probably with a wink to Lyndon, "I know how you've got to have guidelines and rules and I don't want to upset it, but you just go ahead and approve this for me - charge it to my account. I'll gamble on those folks because I've been down in that country and those folks - they'll catch up to that density problem because they breed pretty fast."[206]

Johnson had banked that his special bond with Roosevelt held the key to bringing electricity to the Hill Country. He was right. It was a major coup for a freshman congressman. Johnson had battled the federal bureaucracy, gone head-to-head against clearly defined regulations, and won, but only because he had impressed Roosevelt as "a remarkable young man" in a brief encounter in Texas a year earlier, and only because the president, like the congressman, didn't mind bending the rules when it served his purposes.

"You've got to remember," White House assistant James Rowe, commented "that they were two great political geniuses."[207] Without Roosevelt's direct intervention, it would have been years or even decades before the Hill Country entered the modern world. Twenty years later, Johnson was still immensely proud of his accomplishment: "Of all the things I have ever done, nothing has ever given me as much satisfaction as bringing power to the hill country of Texas."[208]

Having the president's ear was certainly a huge benefit for Johnson's career. Nevertheless, the freshman congressman was also scheming about his future – for the day when Roosevelt wouldn't be president any longer, and when he himself would finally reach his lifelong ambition of moving into the White House as commander-in-chief.

Early in his congressional career, Johnson instructed his aide, Horace Busby, to "refer to him in press releases as LBJ." His strategy was to become known in the public's eye and the media by his initials, just like a president – like TR or FDR. It was part of Johnson's subtle, perceptive, and early efforts to brand himself as somebody. Johnson explained to Busby: "FDR-LBJ, FDR-LBJ – do you get it? What I want is for them to start thinking of me in terms of initials."[209] His presidential ambitions were deeply embedded in his psyche.

A month after the Roosevelt had gone to bat for Johnson and pulled strings to bring electricity to the Hill Country, Johnson began to second guess the relationship. The congressman was anguished when his name did not show up on the list of dignitaries scheduled to ride a train with the President on a campaign swing into Texas. It was part of Roosevelt's political "purge" trip across the country to campaign for congressional candidates who would support his policies, and against incumbent Democrats who had resisted the New Deal. Given Roosevelt's obvious fondness for Johnson, the congressman's paranoia at being left off the guest list had nothing to do with somehow being out of favor with the president. FDR was simply focusing his whistle stop tour on those who needed his support and Johnson, as a Roosevelt stalwart, was running unopposed. Johnson, who just had to be at the center of everything, was nevertheless agitated and worried that he had been left off the list. True to form, he managed to finagle an invitation to ride the presidential train and was publicly praised by Roosevelt. He was disappointed, however, that he wasn't among the chosen few selected to have a private conversation with the President.[210]

Common Agenda
(1939)

The year 1939 would prove to be a significant one for Johnson, as he wormed his way into national politics and into the president's debt for his loyalty. If Oscars were awarded that year for politicians, Johnson would undoubtedly have been a strong contender for Best Supporting Actor. He had an uncanny political sense of sniffing out and creating opportunities to be visible and needed, to exploit leadership vacuums, to promote himself, and to cozy up with the movers and shakers of Washington.

Since he first arrived on Capitol Hill as a congressional secretary, he had cultivated a relationship with Congressman Sam Rayburn. By the time Johnson returned to Washington as a congressman, Rayburn was the House Majority Leader. A life-long bachelor, except for a failed three-month marriage, Mr. Sam had no children, and viewed the deferential young Johnson as the son he never had – something Johnson went to great pains to promote.

In January 1939, less than two years into his congressional career, Johnson engineered an event designed to give him credit for improving ties between the White House and Congress – and at the same time to further solidify his relationship with two of the nation's most influential men – whose last names both started with the letter "R" – Roosevelt and Rayburn.

LBJ suggested to White House aides that Roosevelt should throw a surprise birthday party for Rayburn. Roosevelt "thought it was a great idea."[211] Johnson jumped into action and bought a big Stetson hat with his own money for the president to give to Mr. Sam. Roosevelt played along with the surprise element of the party.

After summoning Rayburn to the Oval Office, FDR sternly announced to the unsuspecting Rayburn: "You are in real trouble and I'm the fellow to tell you…You are the age of [fifty-seven]." At that moment, the Texas congressional delegation, who Johnson had rounded up for the occasion, burst into the room singing "Happy Birthday." In pictures taken of the party, which appeared in the newspapers the following day, Johnson was prominently featured standing between the president and Rayburn.[212] It was a great publicity stunt for the man who just had to be at the center of everything.

While the birthday bash for Rayburn opened the doors of the White House for Lyndon and gave him the chance to rub shoulders with the president, it was only temporary access. It wasn't an effective long-term strategy for building and strengthening his friendship with FDR. He needed something more enduring – something that would make him indispensable to the President. He hoped the success of the Rayburn party was a barometer of his favored status with Roosevelt.

With that in mind, he tried to get back into the Oval Office by writing to the President a few months later. On March 24th, he told FDR some thoughts had come into his mind that "I feel I just have to talk over with the Chief."[213] After such a bold ploy by the freshman congressman to meet with the President of the United States, he struck a properly deferential tone admitting that "I know I can't consume your time,"[214] all the while hoping the President would offer up some of his time. In the letter, he also recommended the president appoint an acquaintance of his for a job. Roosevelt obviously liked Lyndon, but as Johnson understood, the president was a busy man with the weight of the world on his shoulders.

FDR was also a pragmatic politician and there was nothing he needed from Lyndon now. A meeting just wasn't necessary. Johnson's hopes for a friendly chat with Roosevelt were dashed when he received back a form letter from a presidential assistant with no response from the president himself.[215]

The imposing White House doors that had sometimes swung open for him now blocked his access to the President, and he didn't like it. He felt desperate to do or offer something different that would make him stand out from the crowd of the other 530 members of Congress. He brooded about a strategy that would compel the president to beat a path to his door and seek him out.

Like the self-absorbed boy he had been in the Hill Country, he was still driven to be at the center of power. The thought never crossed his mind that having only two years under his belt as a congressman might somehow be a roadblock. He was in a hurry and unwilling to patiently wait for his turn to become a power broker. Instead, he was determined to shape his own future by whatever means he could.

In the summer of 1939, LBJ concocted an ambitious and risky scheme. He volunteered for a dangerous spy mission – not the clandestine foreign type – but a political intelligence mission. Without being asked by anyone, but intuitively sensing a vacuum that begged to be filled, Johnson began to surreptitiously deliver inside information to the White House of the dealings and strategies of Vice President John Nance Garner.

Even though he was FDR's vice president, Garner and Roosevelt were not on the same political page. In fact, the liberal president and conservative Cactus Jack weren't even reading from the same book. Garner was becoming a major obstacle to the New Deal and a threat to a possible third term for Roosevelt, should he decide to run again in 1940. Garner had fought many of FDR's policies, including the Supreme Court packing plan and unbalanced budgets. The relationship between the president and vice president was icy, tense, and far from civil.

It wasn't hard for Johnson to obtain information about Garner's embryonic presidential campaign. The Texas congressional delegation met weekly, and frequently, the topic of discussion centered on how they could promote the aspirations of Garner, a fellow Texan. It was, however, politically perilous for Johnson to operate as a double agent – pretending to be a loyal Texas congressman one moment, and the next furtively slipping news to the White House on Garner's latest shenanigans. However, it was worth the risk for Johnson. He quickly became the president's indispensable link to political intelligence on Garner. White House aide James Rowe remembers that "If we wanted to know something: 'Call Lyndon Johnson'"[216] became the clarion mantra.

Johnson's lowdown on Garner was important for the president in evaluating whether to run for a third term and, more importantly, with how to counteract and deflate the growing Garner boom. Had the Garner machine been left unchecked, Roosevelt would have been operating in the dark and could have lost a strategic political advantage. In the process of demonstrating loyal support to Roosevelt at this critical juncture, Johnson was storing up for himself valuable political capital with the president that would later advance and help keep Johnson's career on track.

Not only did Johnson serve as a mole in the Garner camp, but he also helped the President smooth out an often-troubled relationship with an influential and wealthy Texas supporter of the New Deal. Charles Marsh was the publisher of six Texas newspapers, and Roosevelt needed his financial and editorial support. Marsh wanted to support the president, but the two had to get beyond their large egos and personal clashes of the past.

In July 1939, the publisher and president met in the Oval Office. Rather than face the president alone, Marsh invited Johnson to join him, knowing that Johnson and the president were friends. Marsh liked the freshman congressman who had positioned himself as a professional son to him.

What Marsh didn't know was that the married Johnson was currently carrying on an affair with Marsh's mistress, Alice Glass. Marsh would have been livid about such a betrayal by two of the people closest to him had he known the truth. If Roosevelt had known the secret, he would have winked and been sympathetic with Johnson's dalliance. Years earlier, FDR carried on an illicit affair with Eleanor's social secretary, Lucy Mercer. Despite FDR's promises to his wife that he would break off the relationship, Roosevelt continued to meet with Lucy regularly throughout the rest of his life.

The presidential meeting with Marsh went well, and Roosevelt was once again impressed with this freshman congressman from Texas who seemed to have a knack for knowing everyone and everything.

Two weeks after the White House meeting, a political brouhaha occurred on Capitol Hill that again put Johnson at the center of the stage where he loved to be, and once again in the President's debt. While testifying before a House committee, labor leader John L. Lewis lost his temper, abandoned all political propriety, and lashed into Vice President Garner with some very savage words, colorfully accusing him of being a "labor-baiting, poker-playing, whiskey-drinking, evil old man."[217] The word of the shocking breach of protocol spread quickly throughout Washington.

Garner was outraged when he heard the pointed accusations against him, especially because they had a ring of truth to them. More than that, he was concerned that such inflammatory rhetoric could sink or seriously cripple his presidential aspirations. Garner demanded that Sam Rayburn, the respected dean of the Texas delegation and house majority leader, convene the Texas lawmakers and issue a statement that Lewis' caricature of Garner was patently false.

Before the caucus met, however, Johnson got marching orders from the White House to quash any such resolution from the Texas Democrats. While the president had not yet made up his mind whether to run for a third term, he didn't want to do anything to promote Garner's potential challenge to him. Allowing Lewis' outburst to stand unchecked would be a set-back for Garner.

When the twenty-three-member delegation met, Johnson was still the new kid on the block, having been in Congress just over two years. Ten of his colleagues had been in Congress for over a decade and Sam Rayburn's longevity in the House dated back to when Lyndon was just a four-year-old toddler. During the caucus debate, Johnson stood alone in refusing to agree with the proposed resolution that would condemn Lewis' accusations against Garner. When challenged by his colleagues to explain his insubordination and lack of party and Texas loyalty, he told them that "the delegation will look foolish because everyone knows that Garner is a heavy drinker and that he is bitterly opposed to labor."[218] It was one of the few times Johnson took a stand on the side of truth, although his motivation was more political than principled.

With his control of the delegation at risk, the concerned Rayburn took the young congressman aside into his office to twist his arm and have him back off his opposition to the resolution, but Johnson held his ground. "Lyndon, I am looking you right in the eye," Rayburn said forcefully, hoping to intimidate Lyndon into submission. However, Johnson wasn't about to get pushed around by anyone, even someone like Rayburn, and so he calmly replied to Mr. Sam, without blinking, "And I am looking you right back in the eye."[219] Eventually, a watered down version of the statement that Johnson could agree to was issued.

By itself, Johnson's role in the Lewis-Garner affair wouldn't necessarily have been noteworthy except he was a masterful storyteller and self-promoter, and so he pumped the episode for all it was worth. Lyndon told his account to the White House and anyone else who would listen, describing how he had refused to bend under the pressure of Rayburn and the Texas delegation. Roosevelt loved the story. It demonstrated Lyndon's loyalty, and he re-told it to others. When forced to choose between the two most important father figures in his life, Johnson chose to side with the one who could do him the most good – the more powerful president rather than the house majority leader.

Immediately after the Lewis affair, on the last day of July, Johnson artfully deflected a query from newspaper reporters who were pressing to find out the opinions of the Texas delegation on Garner's presidential bid. Although usually not one to allow his inexperience to stand in his way, on this occasion, Johnson shrewdly stated that "Since the Vice President has not announced his desire to become a candidate for President, I feel an announcement from a new Congressman should await, not precede, his decision."[220]

The president couldn't help but notice that this young Texas boy was an active, loyal, and valuable team player. Johnson took personal risks to provide inside information to the White House on Garner. He facilitated the important meeting for the president with the wealthy and influential publisher Charles Marsh. He stood his ground in the Lewis affair, defeating Garner's attempts to twist the public perception about his drinking habits and "labor-baiting" tactics. And he finessed his way around the question of his support for Garner's presidential ambitions in order not to offend Garner, without really saying who he supported. It was clear to the president – Johnson could be counted on.

Roosevelt recognized that one of his most important tasks was to appoint competent and loyal people to key positions in his administration. Thus, when John Carmody informed the President in 1939 that he would be leaving his position as Administrator of the Rural Electrification Administration, Roosevelt turned his attention to finding an appropriate successor. He didn't have to look far or long before he gratefully offered the job to Johnson, the not-yet 31-year-old congressman. Just four years earlier, Johnson had been an unknown congressional secretary, who had successfully angled his way into a sight-unseen presidential appointment to head the National Youth Administration in Texas. Now he was an increasingly powerful congressman, a loyal friend of the president's, and an important player on the national political stage. Roosevelt was clearly impressed with Johnson.

However, the president's well-intentioned offer to tap Lyndon as REA chief would derail the grandiose long term track that Johnson hoped to ride – a journey he saw leading him from the poor and desolate Hill County to eventually taking up residence at 1600 Pennsylvania Avenue. Had Roosevelt paused long enough to think about it, he would have understood why this wheeler-dealer young man with high ambitions wouldn't want to settle for a job in the federal bureaucracy, even one appointed by the president. FDR liked Lyndon, and wanted to help him however he could, and the REA position was within his power to bestow on his young protégé.

Through his years as a congressional secretary and now as a congressman, Johnson had learned the system on Capitol Hill well. He was his own boss. If he accepted the REA job, he would be reporting to the Secretary of Agriculture (once the REA was reorganized) – and that was simply too far removed from real power for LBJ. And so Johnson, while honored and flattered, graciously wrote to the president on July 29, 1939 to decline the position: "Thanks for your offer to appoint me Administrator of the REA… My own job now, however, is a contract with the people of the Tenth District of Texas, which I hope to complete satisfactorily and to renew every two years as long as I appear useful."[221]

The President responded a few days later with a very complimentary letter, noting the widespread support that Johnson's proposed appointment had garnered from so many quarters. "Dear Lyndon," FDR wrote:

> I was very sorry that you did not feel that you wanted to accept the proffer of the administrator of the Rural Electrification Administration, but I do think I ought to tell you that very rarely have I known a proposed candidate for any position receive such unanimous recommendations from all sources as was the case with you. But I do understand the reasons why you felt that you should stay as a representative of your district. I congratulate the Tenth District of Texas.[222]

Even though he had turned down the position, Johnson was proud to have received such a strong endorsement from the president. It was evidence that the poor boy from the Hill Country was becoming somebody if he was recognized like this by the president of the United States. However,

Roosevelt's complimentary words meant nothing to Johnson's agenda if they did not get shared with a broader audience, so that everyone would know what the president thought about Lyndon. Thus, the ever-diligent marketing genius and brazen self-promoter obtained Roosevelt's permission to release the letter to the press.

If it was clear to the president that he could count on Johnson, the vice president had no such confidence in the congressman. As much as Johnson had tried to be discrete about his double-agent status, Garner had growing suspicions about just how supportive Johnson really was or wasn't of his presidential aspirations. In the rough world of Texas politics, such doubts were often dealt with by quietly stirring up electoral opposition to the troublemaker, causing the suspect to be defeated in the next election. Johnson now stood in the bullseye of Garner's aim.

While Johnson had fought off seven competitors in 1937 to win the special election to the House, in 1938 he ran unopposed – a gift he hoped would be repeated in 1940. Garner had other plans however, and his forces whispered in the ear of the Austin postmaster, Ewell Nalle, to find an opponent for Johnson. Johnson was alarmed when he caught wind of what was brewing.

The simplest solution, in Johnson's mind, turned out not to be that simple. He wanted Nalle fired and replaced with a Roosevelt loyalist. He went to Postmaster General Jim Farley and made his request. However, Farley had been infected with the Garner virus, and he refused to fire Nalle, noting that such a termination would be illegal.

Not willing to take "no" for an answer, and knowing he was the fair-haired boy in the White House, Johnson elevated the issue. He asked presidential staff members to talk with the president, with the result that Roosevelt, after forgetting about the matter once, finally acted as desired before the end of August.

Roosevelt wrote in his own hand: "Tell the Post Office that I want this done right away for Cong. Lyndon Johnson. That it is legal and to send me the necessary papers. Tell Lyndon Johnson that I am doing it."[223] The President was obviously grateful to Johnson for his support, and now it was time for the President to support Johnson. Without the President's protection, the young congressman's career could have ended in 1940 before it really began, if a credible candidate had been found to run against him.

Thanks to Roosevelt's direct intervention, Johnson was now well-positioned. He ran unopposed again in 1940, and thus was able to stay politically afloat for another day. Part audacious dreamer, part devious schemer, and clearly a hard worker, LBJ's roadmap for a greater political future was still on track simply because the president liked the young congressman and was willing to do almost anything to help this Texas boy out, even if it meant stretching the boundaries of protocol along the way.

As Roosevelt's aide, Tommy Corcoran recalled, Roosevelt "was a very down-to-earth politician, and so was Lyndon, and that's why they got along."[224] These two political titans both understood power and loved to use it for their purposes. In addition, neither of them was particularly plagued by any pangs of guilt associated with a slight (or not so slight) bending of established rules to meet their objectives. Ethics, like life for them, was not crisply black or white, but a broad spectrum of various shades of gray they used to sanction and justify their actions.

Thirsting for More Power

(1939 – 1940)

While Johnson's political future in the 1940 election was assured, the president's was less certain in the closing days of 1939. The looming question for FDR was whether he would break with the nation's longstanding tradition and seek an unprecedented third term as president.

Everyone, especially presidential hopefuls, eagerly watched for signals that might disclose his intentions. However, FDR was as silent as a sphinx as he wrestled with his decision. He was genuinely conflicted between, as he noted, his "deep personal desire for retirement on the one hand, and that quiet, invisible thing called 'conscience' on the other."[225]

The growing unrest in Europe and the likelihood of the United States getting reeled into war weighed heavily on him. FDR concluded he was uniquely qualified to guide the nation in this time of crisis and uncertainty.

He was also nervous that there was no Democrat of stature to succeed him. If Vice President Garner was promoted by the voters, Cactus Jack's southern style conservatism would likely dismantle eight years of the New Deal and Roosevelt's legacy as well. FDR increasingly envisioned a third term as an opportunity to consolidate the gains he had accomplished in his New Deal years.

In addition to his sense of duty and concern about a successor, FDR wasn't quite ready to give up the reins of power. He was having too good of a time as President – a job that seemed uniquely matched to his skills and temperament. "He loved the power of the presidency," according to his son, James, "and enjoyed the privileges and prestige of the office enormously."[226]

As much as Roosevelt was of two minds, Garner's announcement on December 18, 1939, that he would run for president, regardless of what Roosevelt did, must have jolted the President. He realized he couldn't put the decision off indefinitely. In addition to their political differences and Garner's increasing public opposition to the President, the two made no effort to conceal their mutual personal dislike. In a cutting reference to Garner's fondness for whiskey, Roosevelt caustically noted in a Cabinet meeting that "I see that the Vice President has thrown his bottle – I mean his hat – into the ring."[227]

If Roosevelt chose to run again, he knew there would be an outcry from many who would accuse him of conspiring to become president (or dictator) for life. It would abolish a tradition as old as the nation itself when George Washington had called it quits after two terms.

The president may have taken comfort and encouragement from Washington's 1788 letter to Lafayette in which the not-yet-president wrote: "I can see no propriety in precluding ourselves from the services of any man who, on some great emergency, shall be deemed universally most capable of serving the public."[228]

Perhaps Washington would have acknowledged that the current state of world affairs was just such an emergency, and that the increasingly unstable world and the safety of the country should not be held hostage to a well-established tradition. Roosevelt hoped the voters would agree should he run again.

The turn of world events in 1939 – with Adolf Hitler's brutal invasions and conquests – had begun to shift the tide of public opinion in favor of a third term. Roosevelt was increasingly viewed as the only man who could navigate the nation through the impending crisis and almost certain war, just as he had charted the course for the country during the Depression. While more than half of the Democrats had opposed a third term in March 1939, by January 1940, 78% of the Democrats wanted to keep FDR in the White House. Correspondingly, Garner's popularity had sunk dramatically. The earlier poll had him as the favored candidate with 45% support, but now he barely registered in double digits, picking up support from just 10%.[229]

Ultimately, it was Hitler who helped Roosevelt make his decision. The early April 1940 plundering of Denmark and Norway by the Nazis convinced Roosevelt of his duty to run for a third term. "I think I'm needed," Roosevelt told his son, James. "And maybe I need it," he smilingly added in a moment of candor.[230] The tide of public opinion was increasingly in Roosevelt's favor as the public realized that Garner didn't have what it took to lead the nation in war. In early April, Roosevelt decisively beat Garner in primaries in Wisconsin and Illinois.

Nevertheless, Garner still had plenty of support in his home state of Texas, enough to potentially embarrass the president when the Democratic Party held their state convention at the end of May. Roosevelt's attitude toward Garner's challenge appears to have shifted a couple of times during the spring months, a not surprising development given FDR's wily instincts and tendency to drift with the political winds that would best serve his interests at the time. At the end of March, FDR sent word through Secretary of the Interior Harold Ickes, that he did not want to contest the Texas delegates with Garner.

There were other factors and motivations were at work in the murky world of Texas politics. They centered around the wheeling and dealing of his "old friend" Lyndon Johnson. Johnson wanted to convince Roosevelt of his supreme loyalty by fighting in Garner's home turf for the president. Johnson saw it as a tactic that would give FDR the sense that he was the only Texas New Deal Democrat who could be trusted.

More importantly, another part of Johnson's strategy was to undermine Sam Rayburn in the president's eyes and cast doubt on whether Mr. Sam was loyal to Roosevelt and could be trusted. If Johnson could wrest control away from Rayburn, a new world of patronage and influence in federal contracts and appointments in Texas would be opened to LBJ, along with the corresponding campaign contributions that would flow from controlling such events. Johnson, along with his Texas mentor and now undersecretary of the interior, Alvin Wirtz, met with the president in early April to convince Roosevelt that they could win Texas away from Garner. Roosevelt apparently gave them his blessing to pursue matters.

Meanwhile Rayburn, caught between his loyalty to Garner and Roosevelt, proposed a compromise resolution to be voted on at the state-wide precinct meetings leading up to the state convention. Under Rayburn's proposal, he tried to balance his longstanding friendship with fellow Texan Garner and his commitment to the president who might tap him for vice president in a third term. Rayburn called for one third of the Texas delegates to the national convention in July to vote for Roosevelt, one third for Garner, and one third for Garner but only on the first ballot.

The Rayburn proposal wasn't good enough for Johnson, who fought for more, and especially to ensure that the Texas delegation didn't come out in favor of trying to stop Roosevelt from pursuing a third term. With Johnson's thick fingerprints all over, along with those of Wirtz and Austin Mayor Tom Miller, they concocted a stronger pro-Roosevelt resolution for consideration by the precincts. This was known as "Harmony Resolution." It condemned

Rayburn's proposal, called for a first ballot vote for Garner as a favorite son, and opposed the "stop Roosevelt" movement.

The president kept in touch with all these developments. He remained concerned about Garner's forces taking control of the convention, especially since the Harmony Resolution was not gathering the necessary traction with the party constituency. The key, FDR suggested, was to get the Democratic Party chairman Myron Blalock on board with the Harmony Resolution. Roosevelt told his aides and Johnson to call Wirtz and have Wirtz convince Blalock.

Wirtz suggested, and the president agreed that an identical telegram should be sent to Blalock and Wirtz that would approve of Garner as a first ballot favorite son candidate with the understanding that the "state convention approve and acclaim [the] administration record and will refuse to be a party to any stop Roosevelt movement."[231] The telegram would come from Sam Rayburn.

With Johnson by his side and on his side throughout the battle for the Texas delegates, Roosevelt suggested that the telegram come from not only Rayburn (representing his compromise resolution), but also Johnson (representing the Harmony Resolution and the president's position). By suggesting Johnson be a party to the telegram, Roosevelt believed from Johnson's swagger, confidence, and inside information that he was more of an influential power in Texas politics than perhaps he really was.

Johnson was delighted with the prominent role suggested by the president. Rayburn, the 58-year-old house minority leader, was not happy. He was offended at the suggestion that he should sign the telegram with a freshman kid congressman more than a quarter century younger than he, even if Johnson was his "professional son."

However, given that the direction came from the president himself, Mr. Sam eventually came around and he joined Johnson at the White House on April 29th to meet with FDR, where they shared with him the contents of the telegram and released copies of it to the media.

According to Interior Secretary Ickes, the president took secret delight taking Rayburn down a notch. Ickes wrote in his diary about the meeting with the president: "When Johnson and Rayburn appeared in the President's office that afternoon, he told them benignly that they had been good little boys and that they had 'papa's blessing.' He treated them as political equals, with the malicious intent of disturbing Sam Rayburn's state of mind. I think that he succeeded."[232]

After all the scheming to get the Texas delegation solidly behind the President at the convention on May 28th, the President pulled the plug at the last hour. He instructed LBJ that "I want you to see the Texas delegation goes for Garner," presumably as just a favorite-son. After all the work for the Harmony Resolution, and the telegram to Blalock, LBJ was taken aback and surprised. "Mr. President, what are you talking about?"

"People are proud of their leaders," FDR responded. "If I go in there and take the people away from their leader – I don't need those votes. I'd rather John Garner have the votes. I want to be magnanimous."[233]

In the end, Garner was anointed as favorite-son and the convention voted to condemn the stop Roosevelt movement. Johnson walked away from the proceedings as the vice chairman of the Texas delegation at the mid-July national convention. He had paved the way to help ensure the president's first ballot victory in Chicago, as the President embarked on his third run for the White House.

Beyond that, Johnson got exactly what he had really wanted: to be seen as the president's man in Texas. Rayburn had wanted to play it safe between FDR and Garner and thus had proposed the compromise, which when compared to Johnson's fervor for the president, came across as pro-Garner and anti-Roosevelt. Rayburn's reputation with the president had also been hurt by his handling of the Lewis affair, and by balking at signing the joint telegram with LBJ. Even though Rayburn agreed with the contents of the telegram, his opposition to signing it with Johnson was viewed as an act of presidential disloyalty. Johnson, on the other hand, had positioned himself as strongly pro-Roosevelt, and he was rewarded with being the one Roosevelt would consult about contracts, appointments, and other matters affecting Texas – not Rayburn or others. "A virtual freshman Representative…is now the acknowledged New Deal spokesman in the Lone Star State," a Washington newspaper reported in early May.[234]

Campaign Cash

(1940)

In the rough and tumble world of Texas politics, Johnson had played an important role in delivering Texas Democrats for FDR's re-nomination, and in the process had come out smelling like a rose, at least to the White House. However, the task of helping re-elect Roosevelt and deliver a Democratic House of Representatives in November was a bigger challenge.

Johnson threw his considerable energies and connections into the 1940 campaign, but not directly for the president. Instead, as he often did, he found a need and power vacuum and filled them, this time forcefully inserting himself into the drive to raise contributions for Democratic congressional candidates. He knew that it would not only help his relationship with Roosevelt, but it might provide FDR with a higher Democratic voter turnout at the polls that could give him the margin he needed to win a third term.

Roosevelt, in his bold gamble for a third term, needed all the help he could get. The mood of the country in the fall of 1940 was not favorable to him. The war in Europe was enough to convince the Democratic Party to place their faith in FDR for a third-term nomination. But the war was a rallying cry of Republicans who feared Roosevelt would lead the nation into the war. Furthermore, there was opposition to FDR breaking the longstanding two-term limitation established by George Washington. Early October polls showed FDR's lead decreasing and Gallup showed Wendell Wilke had pulled even with Roosevelt.[235] Roosevelt might not come out on top. And even if he was re-elected, if he lost control of the House to the Republicans, he knew it would be a very difficult four years, something that could tarnish his legacy.

In October, Rayburn warned FDR that the loss of the House "would tear him to pieces just like it did President Wilson after the Republicans won the House in 1918."[236] It was something Roosevelt was clearly worried about. The Democrats had suffered the loss of 82 seats in 1938. Now, in 1940, some projections indicated that another 60 Democratic seats were at risk, which would be enough to flip control of the House to the Republicans and bestow on Sam Rayburn one of the shortest speakerships on record – from September 16 to early January when the new Congress would convene.

Johnson not only understood the serious problem faced by Democrats, but he had the solution: campaign money, and lots of it. He would personally raise the money and funnel it to Democratic congressional candidates. That would bring out the Democratic vote, maintain the House majority, and help re-elect Roosevelt to a third term.

Money was a big problem to the Democrats who were being significantly outspent by Republicans. The head of the Democratic Congressional Campaign Committee, Patrick Henry Drewry, who had been charged with helping his colleagues fund their campaigns, wasn't helping matters. He was too much of a "country gentleman"[237] to aggressively ask others for money.

Congressman Johnson wasn't shy about shaking the right trees. He had ready access to campaign money – funds he could use to build and consolidate his own political power base and be in the debt of others for helping them. The more he positioned himself as the president's ever loyal ally in Texas, the more control he was receiving over who got government construction contracts in the state, as the White House increasingly deferred such decisions to him – not Rayburn or the state's senators – as their point person in Texas.

The more LBJ steered these contracts to his friends at the construction company of Brown & Root, the more money he had available for any political purpose he wanted. In exchange for his help in directing large contracts to Brown & Root, George Brown had offered his unlimited help to Johnson, reminding Lyndon to tell him "when and where I can return at least a portion of the favors. Remember that I am for you, right or wrong, and it makes no difference if I think you are right or wrong. If you want it, I am for it 100%."[238] This is what Johnson had schemed for, and he didn't forget George Brown's unbridled promise.

First, Johnson had to get himself appointed to some role, preferably a formal one, that would authorize him to raise the money for congressional Democrats. However, Rayburn and Democratic National Committee (DNC) chair Ed Flynn, were wary of giving such an obvious self-promoter and inexperienced congressman as Johnson much, if any of a role in campaign financing. Johnson made several proposals to get formal authority to raise money but was rebuffed at every step.

He asked to be appointed as the official liaison between the Democratic Congressional Campaign Committee and the DNC. At Johnson's behest, Congressman Marvin Jones met with the president on September 14th to propose the idea. Jones followed up with a letter urging Johnson's appointment – not surprisingly a letter that LBJ had drafted. However, despite the Roosevelt-Johnson friendship, Roosevelt didn't like the idea of giving the young congressman such a formal role and nixed the idea of Johnson as a "liaison officer" between the two committees. Even an informal role as proposed by the president wasn't satisfactory to Flynn and Rayburn.

Johnson then tried another tactic to get into the middle of the campaign and collect political IOUs. He wrote FDR on October 1st, asking to fill the vacant secretary position at the DNC, a position from which he could work in raising funds. In his letter, Johnson told Roosevelt his concerns about the campaign:

> My own youth and inexperience may be in error, but I feel tonight that we do stand in danger in the lower house. I know in your wisdom you will work it out...Call on me for anything at any time. P.S. We lost eighty-two seats in 1938. The present forty-five margin gives me the night-sweats at three a.m.[239]

Again, Flynn and Rayburn vetoed the idea. Roosevelt returned to his idea of an unofficial role for Johnson. On October 4th, the President wrote to an aide:

> In the morning will you call up Congressman Lyndon Johnson and tell him that Flynn strongly recommends that we proceed on the original basis as worked out between him and Congressman Drewry which will give Johnson a chance at once to send out the letters which were agreed on, but which made no reference to the President, and that he should do this right away...[240]

The "original basis" was an informal role only - certainly not Johnson's ideal. However, he wanted Rayburn's blessing before proceeding as even an officially unsanctioned fundraiser. Time was running short to turn the campaign around and Mr. Sam was increasingly worried about losing the speakership in a Republican tidal wave. It took until October 13th before an increasingly desperate Rayburn changed his mind and finally pleaded with the president to get Johnson involved in some capacity, formal or informal.

The president, who had wanted Johnson's involvement all along, quickly agreed, noting "That boy has got what's needed."[241] "Tell Lyndon to see me tomorrow."[242]

The next morning was October 14th, just 23 short days until the election, and Johnson joined the president on the second floor of the White House for breakfast to discuss the urgent need for congressional campaign contributions, and LBJ's solutions.

While Johnson did not obtain the formal appointment he desired, he did leave his White House meeting with Roosevelt's blessing for him to assist Democratic campaigns across the nation through the Democratic Congressional Campaign Committee. That was enough for him now.

He immediately flew into action, opening an office that day and placing strategic phone calls to begin raising money to distribute to candidates in the closing days of the campaign. Despite the "country gentleman" Drewry still officially in charge of the committee, Johnson would forcefully make the committee his own organization to dispense campaign funds to candidates he deemed worthy of such support. Johnson had once again found the power vacuum, pulled the appropriate strings – this time with some difficulty – and filled the vacuum with his own organization, creating relationships with congressmen who would be indebted to him for their re-election.

On Sunday, October 27th, LBJ and Rayburn met with the president at the White House to report on the need for more money in some tight House races. Based on that meeting, Roosevelt authorized the DNC to give the Democratic Congressional Campaign Committee $50,000 for these critical races. In the end, the money was never transferred. Johnson raised it himself, along with thousands of other dollars.[243]

On election night, Roosevelt was literally and figuratively sweating as the returns trickled into his home in Hyde Park. At one point, with discouraging election results flowing into the dining room where Roosevelt sat at the table, he ordered everyone, including his family, out of the room as he contemplated his potential defeat. As the returns began to lean toward a third term victory, he re-admitted others to the room.

One of the calls he made was to Lyndon Johnson on a specially installed phone between Hyde Park and Johnson's office. FDR wanted a status report on the congressional races: "How many seats are we going to lose?"

Johnson, who had collected and distributed large sums of money, proudly and ecstatically told the president: "We're not going to lose. We're going to gain."[244] It was a stunning reversal of fortune, gaining five Democratic House seats in an election in which the Democrats had originally been forecast to lose up to fifty seats. Presidential aide James Rowe recalled that "It impressed the hell out of Roosevelt."[245]

After the election, in a follow-up note, Johnson wrote the president to thank him for the opportunity to participate in the campaign in such a significant way. He was properly deferential to the president and downplayed his own role in the victory:

I know some of our Democratic brethren would have been utterly out in the cold except for your good offices. You made it possible for me to get down where I could whiff a bit of the powder, and this note is to say 'Thank You.' It was grand. The victory is perfect.[246]

The president couldn't help but understand that this kid congressman from Texas had saved the day, not only in the House, but in doing so helped FDR win his unprecedented third term. He wrote to Johnson on November 25th to thank him: "I am still getting letters telling me of your fine cooperation in every way, and the results speak for themselves."[247]

Johnson's fundraising had been responsible for maintaining a Democratic majority for the president's third term. Without such a majority, Roosevelt's initiatives would have faced significant resistance. And without such fundraising, the results of the presidential election itself could have taken a different turn. There is a sense in which FDR undoubtedly benefited from a large voter turnout for congressional Democrats, propelling him to re-election.

More importantly for Johnson's career, he was not just an unknown congressman from an isolated district in Texas. He had a significant power base, especially for such a young and new lawmaker. He was beginning to be recognized as a national political figure and a force to be reckoned with. He was the go-to man for the White House, directing contracts to Brown & Root, who in turn would fund not only the 1940 congressional races, but Johnson's future races.

Ballots and Bucks

(1941)

Johnson anticipated that the next campaign when he would need funding from the Brown brothers would be two years off, in which he would run again to represent the voters of the 10th District. However, on April 9, 1941,

Texas senior senator Morris Sheppard suddenly died of a brain hemorrhage at age 65. Sheppard's death presented the politically ambitious Johnson with an opportunity that was too good to pass up. He could run for the vacant position, the next rung up on the career path he had plotted for himself, without having to sacrifice his congressional seat. Almost four years earlier, it had been the death of a long-term Texas congressman that had initially launched Lyndon's congressional career as he had gone on to win the special election to fill the vacant congressional seat.

On April 22nd, less than two weeks after the senator's death, Johnson declared his candidacy for the open senatorial position. It was no ordinary announcement. It didn't take place in Texas or at his congressional office, but on the steps of the White House. Drawing on his special friendship with the president he had forged in less than four years, Johnson went to the White House to confer with the president about the Senate seat and to tell him of his intention to run. He showed Roosevelt the statement he had written. Roosevelt must have been pleased with Johnson's unqualified support, in which the Senate candidate pledged that his "long and consistent record of support of our president will be continued no matter what trials may face us."[248]

Roosevelt suggested that Johnson read his statement right away, immediately before a scheduled presidential press conference. And so the kid congressman threw his hat into the ring at the White House, with the national press corps all present, and the President himself watching and smiling approvingly as his protégé plunged into the race. After Johnson's announcement, reporters covering the event pressed FDR for a statement about Johnson's candidacy. Roosevelt playfully told them:

> I can't take part in a Texas primary…If you ask me about Lyndon himself, I can't take part in his election. I can only say what is perfectly true - you all know he is a very old and close friend of mine. Now that's about all. Now don't try to tie those things together![249]

The President's coy but purposefully transparent remarks brought gales of laughter from the assembled reporters who understood Roosevelt's comments as an informal endorsement of Johnson's long-shot candidacy. During the next two months, Roosevelt did what he could to boost Johnson's chances for success at the polls. "Whatever Johnson wants in terms of projects to be announced, whatever the government can do, they will do it," the president directed his aide, James Rowe.[250]

Johnson's close friendship with the president was well known. During the campaign, Texas Governor W. Lee ("Pappy") O'Daniel, one of the other contenders for the open seat, spoofed Johnson by telling one audience: "You know, that feller Lyndon Johnson is so friendly with the President they tell me he can just walk into the White House and fry his breakfast eggs on the White House stove."[251]

To run a credible campaign in a two-month period and overcome the name identification of his opponents would require lots of cash. For Johnson, campaign money was never an issue. He knew he could rely heavily on his friends at Brown & Root to finance his Senate race. It was, Johnson later acknowledged, a "Brown and Root funded" campaign.[252] Ultimately, neither Johnson's friendship with Roosevelt, the president's personal endorsement, the administration's influence in Texas affairs, nor the perhaps half million dollars poured into the campaign, were enough to overcome the effects of stuffed ballot boxes.

The race was one of the few times in Johnson's political career that he became overconfident, loosening his grip on controlling events just momentarily. On June 28th, the day of the special election, the results were predictable in the counties that Johnson controlled, where he had purchased large blocks of votes: he was significantly ahead, and it looked like he was on his way to taking a Senate seat at just 32.

However, in a moment of strategic weakness and overconfident joy, Johnson let down his guard and gave his approval to publicly release the results of his lead. That was all that Governor O'Daniel's minions needed to know to mysteriously produce votes from counties he controlled to overcome

Johnson's lead. Johnson's heart sank through the next few days as he saw his lead slowly diminish until, from the crowded field of twenty-nine candidates, he finished just 1,311 votes behind O'Daniel. Johnson, who had won previous elections in college and for The Little Congress by questionable election practices, was now the victim himself of stuffed ballot box techniques that were simply more effective than his.

Despite his loss, Johnson was still grateful for the support that Roosevelt had given him. The president's support had brought him within a whisker of victory. Shortly after the election, Johnson wrote the president:

> Sir: In the heat of Texas last week, I said I was glad to be called a water-carrier - that I would be glad to carry a bucket of water to the Commander-in-Chief any time his thirsty throat or his thirsty soul need support, for you certainly gave me support non-pareil. One who cannot arise to the leadership shall find the fault in himself and not in you.[253]

After reading Johnson's note, Roosevelt realized the boy needed some cheering up. He scribbled on the note "I want to see Lyndon" and returned it to his staff to coordinate.[254] When the defeated candidate arrived at the White House on July 29th, he self-righteously complained to Roosevelt that he should have won, but that O'Daniel had stolen the election with stuffed ballot boxes in east Texas, depriving him of his rightful victory. It would have been more accurate for Johnson to explain that O'Daniel had simply done a better job of buying and stealing votes in a delayed manner than Johnson had.

As Roosevelt listened to Johnson's tale of woe, his mind must have gone back a little more than a dozen years earlier to the questionable election practices he witnessed when he was running for governor of New York in 1928, and what he did about them. When vote totals were slow in being reported from upstate New York, he had grown suspicious and called the sheriffs from the counties in question. "This is Franklin Roosevelt," he said.

> I am watching the returns here at the Biltmore Hotel in New York City. The returns from your county are coming in mighty slowly, and I don't like it. I shall look to you, if they are unduly delayed, and I want you personally to see that the ballots are not tampered with. If you need assistance to keep order or to see that the vote is counted right, call me here at this hotel and I shall ask Governor Smith to authorize the state troopers to assist you.[255]

It's something Johnson probably wished he had been able to do in Texas, although it's doubtful that he could use the threat of the governor sending out state troopers to enforce the law. After all, he was running against the governor for the Senate seat.

Roosevelt, like Lyndon, was disappointed with the election loss, but there was nothing that could be done about it. Roosevelt turned to his protégé and teased him saying "Lyndon, apparently you Texans haven't learned one of the first things we learned up in New York State, and that is that when the election is over, you have to sit on the ballot boxes."[256] Roosevelt was still quite fond of this young congressman, and to cheer him up he invited Lyndon to share the national stage with him at the August convention of the Young Democrats by delivering an address just prior to the president's own speech. The meeting with the president was just what Johnson needed. "Had a visit with the Boss today and enjoyed it immensely," he reported to a congressional colleague the next day.[257]

While Roosevelt had not been able to elevate Lyndon into the Senate, he was able to protect him from the political fallout of an IRS investigation into Brown & Root's illegal campaign contributions to Johnson's Senate race. From July 1941 to March 1944, the IRS conducted an extensive investigation into large bonuses paid to Brown & Root employees that ended up in

Johnson's campaign coffers. Johnson and others met with the IRS to get them to halt the investigation, but without success. After conducting interviews with dozens of Brown & Root employees and tracing checks and withdrawals, the IRS had concluded that Brown & Root had underpaid more than $1 million of taxes. When coupled with the fifty percent penalty for cases of fraud, which the IRS believed were justified, Brown & Root's obligation to the government exceeded $1.6 million. If the case went forward, it also meant potential prison time for some Brown & Root employees.

The risks of the investigation to Johnson's embryonic career were monumental. If word of the IRS probe became public and charges were made against Brown & Root, Johnson would not just be mildly tainted, but politically wounded, perhaps fatally, by his association with the scandal. It could effectively put an end to his career. Even if he survived the public relations disaster, conviction of Brown & Root would put an end to his easy campaign cash for his future races. His political base he had built in the 1940 congressional races with Brown & Root money would dry up, along with his power that came with the money. Without the power base, his dream of one day serving in the Senate and eventually becoming president, would evaporate.

In early January 1944, an increasingly worried Johnson requested an immediate appointment with the president, saying that the subject matter he wished to discuss was no "Sunday School proposition."[258] He and Alvin Wirtz, his longtime mentor and Senate campaign manager, finally met with Roosevelt on January 13th to explain the problems of the IRS investigation. Not only would it impact future fund raising and Johnson's career, but it could also politically hurt the President himself who had close ties in the public's eyes with Johnson.

That afternoon, the IRS was ordered to the White House the next day to report on the case. And an IRS agent with no previous involvement with the case was dispatched to Texas to look over the facts, concluding that there was insufficient evidence to prosecute the case. Finally, in early March, the agent in charge of the investigation was directed to close the case. In the end, Brown & Root was ordered to pay just $372,000 with all fraud charges dropped.

Special Feelings

(1937 – 1945)

Roosevelt had intervened on Johnson's behalf, just as he had so many times before, bending rules and protocol to get the desired result. The personal bond between them was founded on mutual admiration, common traits, and a delight in exercising power. At various points over an eight-year span, starting with Johnson's 1937 congressional victory through Roosevelt's death in 1945, the "special feeling"[259] that White House aide James Rowe said existed between the two men was the factor that led each to promote and protect the other. However, there was also a less formal part of their relationship, one in which the two political giants just wanted to talk together. Johnson later recalled that the president would "call me up," and "I used to go down sometimes and have a meal with him."[260]

While they each needed one another, enjoyed one another, and saw themselves reflected in the other, Roosevelt was clearly in the position of greater power and the more polished politician. After all, he had grown up on a privileged patrician estate where refinement was part of everyday life. Johnson, on the other hand, while having the raw appetite for political power like FDR, had a harder time taming it. Like Roosevelt, his background and upbringing also shaped his expression of power, which was more crude and less cultured than Roosevelt's. The extreme poverty of the desolate Hill Country afforded Johnson no model for polish and grace while growing up, and he would always be viewed as somewhat rough-hewn throughout his life.

What did FDR think of this exuberant and political genius of a young man? The nature of their relationship from Roosevelt's perspective is perhaps best characterized by something he wrote to Johnson upon the birth of Johnson's daughter. Shortly after Lynda's arrival on March 19, 1944, the President sent a book about his dog, Fala, to Johnson's home as a baby gift for the newborn. In his own hand, the President had inscribed the book: "From the master – to the pup."[261]

After more than a dozen years as president during some of the most stressful times in the history of the nation, Franklin Roosevelt's weary body finally gave out on April 12, 1945. His death shocked and grieved the nation, many of whom could scarcely remember that anyone else had ever been President. For Congressman Lyndon Johnson, Roosevelt's death was particularly devastating. Ever since Lyndon had returned to Washington as a congressman, he had enjoyed special access to the power of the White House through the natural rapport and friendship that had developed between the two men. Now Johnson's patron was gone, and he felt alone.

On the day of FDR's death, *New York Times* reporter William S. White found a teary-eyed Johnson in the Capitol. With his jaw shaking as he talked, Johnson mournfully processed the impact of his mentor's death. "There are plenty of us left here to try to block and run interference, as he had taught us," Johnson said, "but the man who carried the ball is gone – gone."[262] Johnson continued to talk about Roosevelt as he poured out his grief to White:

He was like a daddy to me, always. He always talked to me just that way. He was the one person I ever knew – anywhere – who was never afraid. Whatever you talked to him about, whatever you asked him for, like projects for your district, there was just one way to figure it with him. I know some of them called it demagoguery; they can call it anything they want, but you can be damn sure that the only test he had was this: Was it good for the folks? They called the President a dictator and some of us they called 'yes' men. Sure, I yessed him plenty of times – because I thought he was right – and I'm not sorry for a single 'yes' I ever gave. I have seen the President in all kinds of moods – at breakfast, at lunch, at dinner – and never once in my five terms did he ever ask me to vote a certain way, or even suggest it. And when I voted against him – as I have plenty of times – he never said a word. I don't know that I'd ever have come to Congress if it hadn't been for him. But I do know that I got my first desire for public office because of him – and so did thousands of other men all over this country.[263]

The President was gone, but his impact on Johnson's career was significant. And as Johnson's grief faded over time, what remained was his gratitude for the influence this man from Hyde Park had on the boy from the Hill Country. Johnson would always remember with fondness his association with the president.

Because all of life was a drama for LBJ with him as a key actor, he took great delight in impersonating the late President who he had idolized. Once, in 1948, he put on a show for a new and unsuspecting congressional aide. He pretended to be FDR as the new aide came into the office, complete with wheeling himself around in a swivel chair, the pince-nez glasses, the patrician voice, the jaw thrust out, and a word-for-word recitation for ten minutes of one of FDR's fireside chats.[264]

The special and mutually beneficial friendship between the longest-serving president and the young Texas congressman significantly shaped both of their careers. FDR was responsible for elevating LBJ to the head of the Texas NYA. He bent the rules to deliver electricity to the Hill Country. He gave Johnson a power base to raise money for Democrats in 1940. And perhaps most significantly, FDR squashed a damaging IRS investigation that would have implicated both FDR and the congressman.

LBJ's contributions to FDR included helping the president win a third term with campaign cash and delivering a Democratic House for the president. Johnson also provided valuable political intelligence to Roosevelt about Garner's presidential aspirations.

Without this friendship, history would have turned out very differently.

Even years after Roosevelt's death, his influence continued to shape Johnson. Once, after LBJ had become President, he stood in the White House admiring a bronze bust of FDR. "*There* was a man," he said. "Look at that chin. Look at how fearless he was. Look at his courage."[265]

NOTES

1. Signed card by Vice President George H.W. Bush to Ruth and Chuck Lieb, June 14, 1986.

2. Richard Norton Smith, *An Uncommon Man, The Triumph of Herbert Hoover* (New York: Simon and Schuster, 1984), p. 421.

3. Bill Clinton, *Remarks and Exchange with Reporters on the Death of President Richard Nixon on April 22, 1994*, pp. 896-897 (Washington, DC: Government Publishing Office, Weekly Compilation of Presidential Documents, Volume 30, Number 17, May 2, 1994). https://www.govinfo.gov/content/pkg/WCPD-1994-05-02/html/WCPD-1994-05-02-Pg896.htm

4. Richard Harwood and Haynes Johnson, *Lyndon* (New York: Praeger Publishers, 1973), p. 36.

5. John Adams to Thomas Jefferson, 15 July 1813, with Postscript from Abigail Adams to Thomas Jefferson, [ca. 15 July 1813], *Founders Online,* National Archives,

   https://founders.archives.gov/documents/Jefferson/03-06-02-0247. [Original source: *The Papers of Thomas Jefferson*, Retirement Series, vol. 6, *11 March to 27 November 1813*, ed. J. Jefferson Looney. Princeton: Princeton University Press, 2009, pp. 296–298.]

6. Gerald R. Ford, *A Time to Heal* (New York: Harper & Row, 1979), p. 414.

7. Don Richardson, ed., *Conversations with Carter* (Boulder: Lynne Rienner Publishers, 1998), p. 23, quoting *U.S. News & World Report*, September 13, 1976 interview with Jimmy Carter.

8. Jimmy Carter, Remarks at the Funeral Service for Gerald R. Ford, January 2, 2007, Delivered at Grace Episcopal Church, Grand Rapids, Michigan.

   https://www.cartercenter.org/news/editorials_speeches/ford_eulogy.html

9. *New York Times*, November 19, 1992, p. A22, "Washington Greets Clinton with Open Arms," by Felicity Barringer.

10. James Langland, editor, *The Chicago Daily News Almanac and Year-Book for 1919.* Woodrow Wilson speech on May 18, 1918 at the Metropolitan Opera house in New York City for Red Cross fundraising event. (Chicago: The Chicago Daily News Company, 1918), p. 406.

https://www.google.com/books/edition/The_Chicago_Daily_News_Almanac_and_Yearb/f6l-dsvnjhEC?hl=en&gbpv=1&dq=%22Friendship+is+the+only+cement%22&pg=PA406&printsec=frontcover

11.   Judith Icke Anderson, *William Howard Taft, An Intimate History* (New York: W.W. Norton & Company, 1981), p. 59.

12.   Judith Anderson, *Taft, An Intimate History*, p. 59.

13.   Henry F. Pringle, *The Life and Times of William Howard Taft*, Volume I (New York: Farrar & Rinehart, Inc., 1939), p. 107.

14.   Judith Anderson, *Taft, An Intimate History*, pp. 58-59.

15.   Nathan Miller, *Theodore Roosevelt, A Life* (New York: William Morrow and Company, Inc., 1992), p. 204.

16.   Miller, *Theodore Roosevelt, A Life*, p. 205.

17.   Judith Anderson, *Taft, An Intimate History*, p. 59.

18.   Oscar King Davis, *William Howard Taft, The Man of the Hour* (Philadelphia: P.W. Ziegler Co., 1908), p. 10.

19.   W. H. Michael, Clerk of Printing Records, *1890 Official Congressional Directory* (corrected as of December 3, 1890). (https://books.google.com/books/about/Serial_set_no_0_3099.html?id=K4w3AQAAIAAJ). Roosevelt resided in a row house at 1820 Jefferson Place NW, Washington, DC from 1889 until around 1892. Taft lived in a townhouse at 5 Dupont Circle (since demolished). Their homes in the same neighborhood were about a half-mile apart. TR's office was in City Hall at 451 Indiana Ave. NW (p. 194), while Taft's were on Pennsylvania Ave between 15th and 16th Streets (p. 192).

20.   Judith Anderson, *Taft, An Intimate History*, p. 59.

21.   H. Wayne Morgan, *William McKinley and His America* (Syracuse, New York: Syracuse University Press, 1963), p. 262.

22.   Edmund Morris, *The Rise of Theodore Roosevelt* (New York: Coward, McCann & Geoghegan, Inc., 1979) p. 551.

23.   Miller, *Theodore Roosevelt, A Life*, p. 246.

24.   April 5, 1897.

25.   Donald F. Anderson, *William Howard Taft, A Conservative's Conception of the Presidency* (London: Cornell University Press, 1968), pp. 8-9.

26.   Donald F. Anderson, *Taft, A Conservative's Conception of the Presidency*, pp. 8-9.

27.   Donald F. Anderson, *Taft, A Conservative's Conception of the Presidency*, p. 9.

28.   Paolo E. Coletta, *The Presidency of William Howard Taft* (Lawrence: The University Press of Kansas, 1973), p. 6.

29.   Ishbel Ross, *An American Family, The Tafts – 1678 to 1964* (Cleveland, Ohio: The World Publishing Company, 1964), p. 140. October 21, 1901 letter.

30.   David C. Whitney, *The American Presidents* (Garden City, New York: Doubleday & Company, Inc., 1978) p. 232.

31.   Ross, *An American Family*, p. 145. Delivered to the pope in June 1902.

32.   Donald F. Anderson, *Taft, A Conservative's Conception of the Presidency*, p. 5.

33.   *Telegram from Theodore Roosevelt to William H. Taft*. Theodore Roosevelt Papers. Library of Congress Manuscript Division. https://www.theodore-rooseveltcenter.org/Research/Digital-Library/Record?libID=o183389. Theodore Roosevelt Digital Library. Dickinson State University.

34.   Donald F. Anderson, *Taft, A Conservative's Conception of the Presidency*, p. 10.

35.   *Telegram from William H. Taft to Theodore Roosevelt*. Theodore Roosevelt Papers. Library of Congress Manuscript Division. https://www.theodore-rooseveltcenter.org/Research/Digital-Library/Record?libID=o39565. Theodore Roosevelt Digital Library. Dickinson State University.

36.   Donald F. Anderson, *Taft, A Conservative's Conception of the Presidency*, p. 10.

37.   *Letter from Theodore Roosevelt to William H. Taft*. Theodore Roosevelt Papers. Library of Congress Manuscript Division. https://www.theodoreroos-eveltcenter.org/Research/Digital-Library/Record?libID=o266192. Theodore Roosevelt Digital Library. Dickinson State University.

38.   Tim Taylor, *The Book of Presidents* (New York: Arno Press, 1972), p. 313.

39.   Harry F. Pringle, *The Life and Times of William Howard Taft*, Volume 1 (New York: Farrar & Rinehart, Inc., 1939), p. 245.

40.   Mrs. William Howard Taft, *Recollections of Full Years* (New York: Dodd, Mead & Company, 1914), p. 269.

41.   Pringle, *Life and Times of Taft*, Volume 1, p. 244.

42.   Brands, *TR: The Last Romantic*, p. 596.

43.   Ross, *An American Family*, p. 150.

44.   Mrs. Taft, *Recollections of Full Years*, p. 269.

45.   Pringle, *Life and Times of Taft*, p. 254.

46.   Ross, *An American Family*, p. 151.

47.   *Letter from Theodore Roosevelt to Theodore Roosevelt*. Theodore Roosevelt Papers. Library of Congress Manuscript Division. https://www.theodore-rooseveltcenter.org/Research/Digital-Library/Record?libID=o187311. Theodore Roosevelt Digital Library. Dickinson State University.

48. Pringle, *Life and Times of Taft*, p. 259.

49. Pringle, *Life and Times of Taft*, p. 259.

50. Ross, *An American Family*, p. 160.

51. *Letter from Theodore Roosevelt to Leonard Wood.* Theodore Roosevelt Papers. Library of Congress Manuscript Division. https://www.theodorerooseveltcenter.org/Research/Digital-Library/Record?libID=o188312. Theodore Roosevelt Digital Library. Dickinson State University.

52. Donald F. Anderson, *Taft, A Conservative's Conception of the Presidency*, p. 14.

53. Donald F. Anderson, *Taft, A Conservative's Conception of the Presidency*, p. 15.

54. Donald F. Anderson, *Taft, A Conservative's Conception of the Presidency*, p. 16.

55. Donald F. Anderson, *Taft, A Conservative's Conception of the Presidency*, p. 17.

56. Donald F. Anderson, *Taft, A Conservative's Conception of the Presidency*, p. 16.

57. Donald F. Anderson, *Taft, A Conservative's Conception of the Presidency*, pp. 16-17.

58. Brands, *TR: The Last Romantic*, p. 596.

59. Coletta, *Presidency of Taft*, p. 6.

60. Judith Anderson, *Taft, An Intimate History*, p. 91.

61. Judith Anderson, *Taft, An Intimate History*, p. 91.

62. Miller, *Theodore Roosevelt, A Life*, p. 434.

63. Miller, *Theodore Roosevelt, A Life*, p. 436.

64. Henry F. Pringle, *Theodore Roosevelt, A Biography* (New York: Harcourt, Brace and Company, 1956), p. 251.

65. Coletta, *Presidency of Taft*, p. 7.

66. Judith Anderson, *Taft, An Intimate History*, p. 91.

67. Miller, *Theodore Roosevelt, A Life*, p. 483.

68. Judith Anderson, *Taft, An Intimate History*, p. 92.

69. Brands, *TR: The Last Romantic*, p. 628.

70. Pringle, *Life and Times of Taft*, p. 356.

71. Brands, *TR: The Last Romantic*, p. 629.

72. Ross, *An American Family*, p. 199.

73. Ross, *An American Family*, p. 200.

74. Ross, *An American Family*, p. 201. Time Magazine Special on Presidents,

under Taft article.

75.   Edmund Morris, *Theodore Rex* (New York: Random House, 2001), p. 528.

76.   Ross, *An American Family*, p. 203.

77.   Pringle, *Theodore Roosevelt, A Biography*, p. 357, quoting Roosevelt's December 31, 1908 letter to Taft.

78.   Ross, *An American Family*, p. 206.

79.   On Taft's last day as President, as he prepared to turn the reins of government over to Woodrow Wilson in 1913, he lamented to the new president that "this is the loneliest place in the world."

80.   Ross, *An American Family*, p. 203.

81.   Judith Anderson, *Taft, An Intimate History*, p. 208.

82.   Ross, *An American Family*, p. 211.

83.   Ross, *An American Family*, p. 207.

84.   Paul F. Boller, Jr., *Presidential Inaugurations* (New York: Harcourt, Inc., 2001), p. 234.

85.   Boller, *Presidential Inaugurations*, p. 234.

86.   Boller, *Presidential Inaugurations*, pp. 70-71

87.   Boller, *Presidential Inaugurations*, pp. 70-71.

88.   Mrs. Taft, *Recollections of Full Years*, p. 331.

89.   John Callan O'Laughlin, "Roosevelt Gay as Boy Out of School," *Los Angeles Times*, March 4,1909.

90.   Judith Anderson, *Taft, An Intimate History*, p. 119.

91.   Judith Anderson, *Taft, An Intimate History*, p. 207.

92.   John J. Leary, Jr., *Talks with T.R.* (Boston: Houghton Mifflin Company, 1920), pp. 25-26.

93.   Judith Anderson, *Taft, An Intimate History*, p. 124.

94.   Judith Anderson, *Taft, An Intimate History*, p. 124.

95.   Judith Anderson, *Taft, An Intimate History*, p. 124.

96.   Judith Anderson, *Taft, An Intimate History*, p. 209.

97.   Ross, *An American Family*, p. 241.

98.   Judith Anderson, *Taft, An Intimate History*, p. 207.

99.   Judith Anderson, *Taft, An Intimate History*, p. 207.

100.   Judith Anderson, *Taft, An Intimate History*, p. 207.

101.   Ross, *An American Family*, p. 239.

102.   Judith Anderson, *Taft, An Intimate History*, p. 213.

103.   Philip B. Kunhardt, Jr., Philip B. Kunhardt III, Peter W. Kunhardt, *The*

American President (New York: Riverhead Books, 1999), p. 420.

104. James Chace, *1912: Wilson, Roosevelt, Taft & Debs – The Election That Changed the Country* (New York: Simon & Schuster Paperbacks, 2004), pp. 34-35.

105. Brands, *TR: The Last Romantic*, p. 672.

106. Donald F. Anderson, *Taft, A Conservative's Conception of the Presidency*, pp. 176-177. August 19, 1910 letter of President Taft to Major Archie Butts.

107. Judith Anderson, *Taft, An Intimate History*, p. 216. Roosevelt's trip was from August 23 to Sept 11, 1910.

108. Ross, *An American Family*, p. 240. Taft's September 10, 1910 letter to his brother, Charles.

109. Ross, *An American Family*, p. 240. Taft's September 10, 1910 letter to his brother, Charles.

110. Judith Anderson, *Taft, An Intimate History*, p. 223.

111. Donald F. Anderson, *Taft, A Conservative's Conception of the Presidency*, p. 156. September 1910.

112. Judith Anderson, *Taft, An Intimate History*, p. 215.

113. Judith Anderson, *Taft, An Intimate History*, p. 221.

114. Judith Anderson, *Taft, An Intimate History*, p. 127.

115. Judith Anderson, *Taft, An Intimate History*, p. 127.

116. Judith Anderson, *Taft, An Intimate History*, p. 125.

117. William A. Degregorio, *The Complete Book of U.S. Presidents* (New York: Wings Books, 1993), p. 405.

118. Judith Anderson, *Taft, An Intimate History*, pp. 219-220.

119. Miller, *Theodore Roosevelt, A Life*, p. 518.

120. Donald F. Anderson, *Taft, A Conservative's Conception of the Presidency*, p. 273.

121. Judith Anderson, *Taft, An Intimate History*, p. 220.

122. Judith Anderson, *Taft, An Intimate History*, p. 221.

123. Judith Anderson, *Taft, An Intimate History*, p. 224.

124. Elizabeth Frost, editor, *The Bully Pulpit, Quotations from America's Presidents* (New York: New England Publishing Associates, Inc., 1988), p. 235. August 1911.

125. Coletta, *Presidency of Taft*, pp. 224-225. October 27, 1911.

126. Brands, *TR: The Last Romantic*, p. 698. December, 1911.

127. Joseph Bucklin Bishop, *Theodore Roosevelt and His Time, Shown in His Own Letters*, Volume II (New York: Charles Scribner's Sons, 1920), p. 313.

128. Donald F. Anderson, *Taft, A Conservative's Conception of the Presidency*, p. 179.

129. Kunhardt, *The American President*, p. 420.

130. Judith Anderson, *Taft, An Intimate History*, p. 224.

131. Coletta, *Presidency of Taft*, p. 223. Taft writing to his friend Otto T. Bannard, January 22, 1912.

132. Pringle, *Life and Times of Taft*, p. 766.

133. Miller, *Theodore Roosevelt, A Life*, p. 441.

134. Judith Anderson, *Taft, An Intimate History*, p. 90.

135. Judith Anderson, *Taft, An Intimate History*, p. 250.

136. Coletta, *Presidency of Taft*, p. 227.

137. Pringle, *Life and Times of Taft*, p. 781. April 25, 1912.

138. Pringle, *Life and Times of Taft*, p. 782. April 25, 1912.

139. Brands, *TR: The Last Romantic*, p. 712.

140. *Presidential History Magazine*, July 1998, p. 28.

141. Pringle, *Life and Times of Taft*, p. 771. April 1, 1912.

142. Pringle, *Life and Times of Taft*, p. 771. April 10, 1912.

143. Pringle, *Life and Times of Taft*, p. 775.

144. Kunhardt, *The American President*, p. 422.

145. Brands, *TR: The Last Romantic*, p. 712.

146. Brands, *TR: The Last Romantic*, p. 712.

147. Francis Russell, *The Shadow of Blooming Grove, Warren G. Harding in His Times* (New York: McGraw-Hill Book Company, 1968), p. 224.

148. Russell, *Shadow of Blooming Grove*, p. 225.

149. *Presidential History Magazine*, July 1998, p. 16.

150. Ross, *An American Family*, p. 258.

151. Judith Anderson, *Taft, An Intimate History*, p. 250.

152. Frost, *The Bully Pulpit*, p. 235.

153. Kunhardt, *The American President*, p. 422.

154. Ross, *An American Family*, pp. 258-259.

155. Frost, *The Bully Pulpit*, p. 235.

156. Miller, *Theodore Roosevelt, A Life*, p. 529.

157. Ross, *An American Family*, p. 258. July 21, 1912.

158. Pringle, *Life and Times of Taft*, p. 771.

159. Judith Anderson, *Taft, An Intimate History*, p. 257.

160. Judith Anderson, *Taft, An Intimate History*, p. 257.

161. Judith Anderson, *Taft, An Intimate History*, p. 257.

162. Judith Anderson, *Taft, An Intimate History*, p. 258.

163. Ross, *An American Family*, p. 308.

164. Ross, *An American Family*, p. 308.

165. Ross, *An American Family*, pp. 307-308.

166. Judith Anderson, *Taft, An Intimate History*, p. 258.

167. Russell, *Shadow of Blooming Grove*, p. 302.

168. Miller, *Theodore Roosevelt, A Life*, p. 559.

169. Judith Anderson, *Taft, An Intimate History*, p. 258.

170. Doris Kearns, *Lyndon Johnson and the American Dream* (New York: The New American Library, Inc., 1977), p. 43.

171. Robert A. Caro, *The Years of Lyndon Johnson: The Path to Power* (New York: Alfred A. Knopf, 1982), p. 100.

172. Caro, *Path to Power*, p. 223.

173. From President Herbert Hoover's speech on January 4, 1932 to a Joint Session of Congress.

    http://www.southalabama.edu/history/faculty/hulse/HerbertHooveronthe-eEconomicCrisis.pdf

174. Caro, *The Path to Power*, p. 223.

175. Caro, *The Path to Power*, p. 229.

176. Kearns, *Johnson and the American Dream*, p. 77.

177. Alfred Steinberg, *Sam Johnson's Boy: A Close-up of the President from Texas* (New York: The Macmillan Company, 1968), p. 75.

178. James M. McPherson, General Editor, *"To The Best of My Ability," The American Presidents* (New York: Dorling Kindersley Publishing, Inc., 2000), p. 232.

179. James Roosevelt with Bill Libby, *My Parents: A Differing View* (Chicago: Playboy Press, 1976), p. 142.

180. Robert Dallek, *Lone Star Rising, Lyndon Johnson and His Times, 1908-1960* (New York: Oxford University Press, 1991), p. 123.

181. Caro, *The Path to Power*, p. 45.

182. Caro, *The Path to Power*, p. 340.

183. Steinberg, *Sam Johnson's Boy*, p. 98.

184. Steinberg, *Sam Johnson's Boy*, pp. 106-107.

185. Caro, *The Path to Power*, p. 390.

186. Caro, *The Path to Power*, p. 446.

187. Presidents Johnson knew: Franklin Roosevelt, Harry Truman, Dwight Eisenhower, John Kennedy, Richard Nixon, Gerald Ford, George H.W. Bush.

188. Caro, *The Path to Power*, p. 447.

189. Steinberg, *Sam Johnson's Boy*, p. 119.

190. Merle Miller, *Lyndon: An Oral Biography* (New York: G.P. Putnam's Sons, 1980), p. 63.

191. Miller, *Lyndon: An Oral Biography*, p. 63.

192. Steinberg, *Sam Johnson's Boy*, p. 119.

193. Steinberg, *Sam Johnson's Boy*, pp. 119-120.

194. Miller, *Lyndon: An Oral Biography*, p. 63.

195. Dallek, *Lone Star Rising*, p. 161.

196. Caro, *The Path to Power*, p. 449.

197. Steinberg, *Sam Johnson's Boy*, p. 121.

198. Caro, *The Path to Power*, p. 526.

199. Caro, *The Path to Power*, p. 524.

200. Steinberg, *Sam Johnson's Boy*, p. 132.

201. H.W. Brands, *Traitor to His Class: The Privileged Life and Radical Presidency of Franklin Delano Roosevelt* (New York: Doubleday, 2008), pp. 354-355.

202. Steinberg, *Sam Johnson's Boy*, p. 132.

203. Steven O'Brien, *American Political Leaders: From Colonial Times to the Present*, Volume 52 (Santa Barbara, California: ABC-CLIO, Inc., 1991), p. 222.

204. Dallek, *Lone Star Rising*, p. 180.

205. Steinberg, *Sam Johnson's Boy*, p. 132.

206. Dallek, *Lone Star Rising*, p. 181.

207. Robert A. Caro, *The Years of Lyndon Johnson: Master of the Senate* (New York: Alfred A. Knopf, 2002), p. 163.

208. Dallek, *Lone Star Rising*, p. 183.

209. Caro, *Master of the Senate*, p. 111.

210. Caro, *The Path to Power*, p. 571.

211. Dallek, *Lone Star Rising*, p. 166.

212. Dallek, *Lone Star Rising*, p. 166.

213. Caro, *The Path to Power*, p. 555.

214. Caro, *The Path to Power*, p. 555.

215. Caro, *The Path to Power*, p. 555.

216. Caro, *The Path to Power*, p. 571.

217. Irwin Unger and Debi Unger, *LBJ, A Life* (New York: John Wiley & Sons, Inc., 1999), p. 86.

218. Steinberg, *Sam Johnson's Boy*, p. 136.

219. Unger, *LBJ, A Life*, p. 87.

220. Caro, *The Path to Power*, p. 574.

221. Caro, *The Path to Power*, p. 577.

222. Caro, *The Path to Power*, p. 577.

223. Caro, *The Path to Power*, p. 575.

224. Miller, *Lyndon: An Oral Biography*, p. 78.

225. July 19, 1940 message of Franklin D. Roosevelt to Democratic National Convention.

    http://millercenter.org/president/speeches/detail/3318

226. James Roosevelt, *My Parents: A Differing View*, p. 162.

227. Caro, *The Path to Power*, p. 572.

228. CQ Press, quoting Secretary of the Interior Harold Ickes in the June 20, 1939 issue of *Look magazine who was quoting George Washington about his thoughts on a third term*: Website: http://library.cqpress.com/cqresearcher/document.php?id=cqresrre1939061900&PHPSESSID=69km1h9t9kfhu0ha-o4tovq8si2

229. Miller, *FDR: An Intimate History*, p. 446.

230. James Roosevelt, *My Parents: A Differing View*, p. 163.

231. Unger, *LBJ, A Life*, p. 90.

232. Caro, *The Path to Power*, p. 593.

233. Randall B. Woods, *LBJ: Architect of American Ambition* (New York: Free Press, A Division of Simon & Schuster, Inc., 2006), p. 143.

234. Caro, *The Path to Power*, p. 598.

235. Caro, *The Path to Power*, p. 625.

236. Caro, *The Path to Power*, p. 625.

237. Caro, *The Path to Power*, p. 607.

238. Caro, *The Path to Power*, p. 606.

239. Dallek, *Lone Star Rising*, p. 199.

240. Caro, *The Path to Power*, p. 621.

241. Unger, *LBJ, A Life*, p. 92.

242. Caro, *The Path to Power*, p. 625.

243. Caro, *The Path to Power*, p. 647.

244. Dallek, *Lone Star Rising*, p. 205.

245. Caro, *The Path to Power*, p. 654.

246. Dallek, *Lone Star Rising*, p. 205.

247. Unger, *LBJ, A Life*, p. 94.

248. Associated Press, "Lyndon B. Johnson, Houston, Enters Race for U.S. Senate," *Borger Daily Herald* (Borger, Texas), April 23, 1941, p. 6, http://texashistory.unt.edu/ark:/67531/metapth168264/m1/6/zoom/.

249. Dallek, *Lone Star Rising*, p. 209.

250. Unger, *LBJ, A Life*, p. 98.

251. Steinberg, *Sam Johnson's Boy*, p. 166.

252. Unger, *LBJ, A Life*, p. 101.

253. Robert A. Caro, *The Years of Lyndon Johnson: Means of Ascent* (New York: Alfred A. Knopf, 1990), p. 10.

254. Caro, *The Path to Power*, p. 742.

255. Brands, *Traitor to His Class*, p. 215.

256. Caro, *Means of Ascent*, p. 10.

257. Caro, *The Path to Power*, p. 742.

258. Caro, *The Path to Power*, p. 751.

259. Caro, *Master of the Senate*, p. 163.

260. Caro, *Master of the Senate*, p. 163.

261. Dallek, *Lone Star Rising*, p. 265.

262. Miller, *Lyndon – An Oral Biography*, p. 104.

263. Richard Harwood and Haynes Johnson, *Lyndon* (New York: Praeger Publishers, 1973), p. 36.

264. Caro, *Master of the Senate*, p. 125.

265. Hugh Sidey, *Portraits of the Presidents* (New York: TIME Books, 2000), p. 4.

ABOUT THE AUTHOR

MIKE PURDY is a presidential historian and the founder of PresidentialHistory.com. He writes, speaks, and podcasts on presidential history and politics.

He is the author of *101 Presidential Insults: What They Really Thought About Each Other – and What It Means to Us*. This well-received 2019 book is available from Amazon, Barnes & Noble, and local bookstores.

PresidentialHistory.com includes an award-winning blog (PR Newswire for Journalists, Beyond Bylines selected it as their top "Presidential Blogs We Love" in February 2018). In addition to resources about presidential sites, books, and various links, his website includes a popular Presidential History News video series. These short and fun videos recreate and imagine what it would look like if a modern television news anchor reported on key events in presidential history.

Mike has been interviewed by and quoted in a variety of national and international media outlets including CNN, *The New York Times*, *The Wall Street Journal*, *USA Today*, *Reader's Digest*, Today.com, Bloomberg BNA, HuffPost, and BBC. He is an opinion contributor to TheHill.com and History News Network.

He is a member of the Organization of American Historians and the American Historical Association. He participated in the Siena College Research Institute's 2018 and 2022 Survey of U.S. Presidents, ranking presidential performance.

Mike has undergraduate and graduate degrees in business administration (University of Puget Sound), and a Master of Divinity degree (Fuller Theological Seminary).

Sign up for a free email subscription to Mike's Presidential History Blog at PresidentialHistory.com.

Follow Mike on:
Twitter @PresHistory
Instagram @PresidentialHistorian

The author can be reached by email at Mike@PresidentialHistory.com.

MIKE PURDY'S
PRESIDENTIALHISTORY.COM